Praise for Wendy Burns and UNMASK: Stop Hiding, Start Living

Get ready to be inspired! This book invites us to break free, shed our masks, and step out of the dark into the light so that we can begin the transformation from within. Unmask: Stop Hiding, Start Living is not only a powerful book but an inspiring one as well. It highlights resilience, hope, and a sense of purpose.

Wendy's story of unmasking her own brokenness and allowing herself to be put back together is an example anyone can draw inspiration from. We are reminded that miracles can happen when we allow God to work in our lives by healing our deepest wounds.

Wendy provides valuable insight that can be applied to anyone's life. You'll discover encouragement as you climb the mountain of 'unmasking' yourself and embracing your true self through her purpose-driven message of faith, hope, and self-leadership.

Vessels that are broken are valuable. Why? This is because our heavenly Father, through His tender love and mercy, repairs broken vessels and skilfully assembles them into a masterpiece. By means of this masterpiece, He can spread His grace and healing to many others.

Thank you, Wendy, for sharing your vulnerable self. There is no doubt that this "remark" and your powerful story and wisdom will impact the lives of millions of people who come across this book.

If you've just picked up this book and are someone in need of hope for your own journey of self-discovery, Unmask: Stop Hiding, Start Living is the book for you. Wendy's story will move you and give you invaluable insight into faith, love, and self-leadership. It is truly a remarkable book!

Unmask: Stop Hiding, Start Living deserves 5 stars and comes highly recommended from me!

Christopher Sajnendra - Coach to CEOs and Entrepreneurs

Leadership, People, and Culture Consultant | Speaker | Author | Pharmacist

"After not being able to put Remarkable You down, I wasn't sure how a second book could exceed it, and yet, I am thrilled to be proven wrong. Wendy epitomizes "Courage in Action." The practical learnings to enhance and support people's lives, coupled with compelling, honest stories woven with thought-provoking and meaningful anecdotes and quotes, makes *Unmask – Stop Hiding, Start Living*" the life toolkit you'll pick up time and time again."

"Wendy has selflessly shared her harrowing yet courageous story to encourage others to acknowledge that "you can't pour from an empty cup, but small actions often will lead to great, positive change."

Rebecca Forrest

2022 NT Local Hero Australian of the Year

By way of background, Wendy Burns was my manager and work colleague for approximately nine (9) years from mid-2002 in an enforcement unit of a Queensland Government Department. Wendy refers to "camouflaging" in this book, and I must admit she did it well in the nine years I worked with her. None of us in that unit knew of what Wendy's "history" (for want of a term) was, this was held close to her chest. I only became aware of Wendy's life when I heard her speak at a Women's Breakfast for a church I attend (I was a volunteer assisting for the day). I nearly cried not only what had occurred in her formative years but with knowing how Wendy had been maliciously vilified in the workplace.

This book along with its predecessor "Remarkable You" are written from the heart, this is Wendy's "story," the journey she had, the demons she confronted, the choices she made not to allow these demons to rule her life, the changes she made to become the "Remarkable Wendy." Wendy's desire is that no matter who reads the book(s) will look in the mirror, do hard soul searching and make the positive choice to kick whatever demons are holding you back and allow you to become the "remarkable you that you are."

The book does not use any fancy terms that psychologists may use, the book is simplistic, and this is not derogatory, it is written from the heart. The book has been written by a person who has "done (and is doing) the hard yards of life" more than most of us potentially will ever do. Wendy has written it with the ultimate hope that she can help at least one person realize their personal "remarkable you." A reader can pick the book up, understand the scenarios presented, and reflect on the suggested actions, leaving the ultimate choices to themselves.

Wendy refers to camouflaging, how we are good at conveying an outward appearance to hide what is lying below the surface in those secret spaces that we protectively guard. In another section, Wendy refers to two birds, the vulture, and hummingbird, each has a different perspective on what it sees. This will make you think of your attitudes.

This book and its predecessor show what Wendy was confronted with, how the scenarios finally brought her to the edge of the cliff where there were ultimately two choices, either the expectation to jump off or to turn around, tackle the entrenched obstacles, root them out and not let them "run" her life. Thankfully Wendy turned around and, through her life experiences, is trying to help others.

David Lambert

From hopelessness to hope, despair, and suicidal thoughts to a woman of influence.

An inspirational read for those who can see no future or purpose for their life.

Wendy's story is remarkable as she shares how she overcame the circumstances of her life to become the woman she is today.

Vicki McLachlan

Raw, authentic, honest, hopeful, encouraging and practical. This book will place you on a path of healing and redemption and I am so happy it has found its way into your hands. I recommend you spoil yourself with a special new journal that will be especially used for this beautiful journey of healing you are about to embark on. It will be life changing and it will be challenging, but I can confidently say that you will not feel alone. As you read this book it's as though Wendy is walking alongside you not just as a coach with all her wisdom and excellent action steps, but also as a loving friend who knows your struggles, sees your pain and will encourage you to keep preserving.

I believe you will feel safe as you read this book. The way Wendy shares and challenges her readers is done in a very careful, thoughtful and gentle way. This book truly puts the power of change into your hands and that in itself is incredibly empowering! If you come to a place while reading this book and you feel like this journey is too hard to travel, just stop and take a breath and when you are ready , continue with a strong and courageous heart. You are not alone. This book has found its way into your hand because you are ready to stop hiding and start living..

Raquel Twigg review for UNMASK Stop Hiding Start Living

UNMASK
STOP HIDING START LIVING

Written by

Wendy Burns

www.wendyburnsconsulting.com.au

Atlanta | Punta del Este

Copyright © 2023 Wendy Burns

www.wendyburnsconsulting.com.au

Published by Skinny Brown Dog Media

Atlanta, GA/Punta del Este, Uruguay

www.SkinnyBrownDogMedia.com

Skinny Brown Dog Media supports copyright. Copyright fuels creativity, encourages diverse voices, promotes free speech, and creates a vibrant culture. Thank you for buying an authorized edition of this book and for complying with copyright laws by not reproducing, scanning, or distributing any part of it in any form without permission. You are supporting writers and allowing Skinny Brown Dog Media to continue to publish books for amazing readers like you.

Distributed by Skinny Brown Dog Media

Design and composition by Skinny Brown Dog Media

Cover Design by Skinny Brown Dog Media

Interior Layout Design by farhanshahid101

Library of Congress Cataloging-in-Publication Data Print

UNMASK: Stop Hiding and Start Living

Journal UNMASK: Stop Hiding and Start Living

eBook ISBN: 978-1-957506-38-8

Hardback ISBN: 978-1-957506-39-5

Paperback ISBN: 978-1-957506-40-1

Companion journal: 978-1-957506-41-8

Every effort has been made to locate and credit the copyright owners of material and quotes in this book. If any sources have not been credited, please call this to our attention, and we will make every effort to correct this in future printings.

Dedication

I dedicate this book to my two precious sisters, Carol and Shirley Kerri, who did not know how to make it through their wounds...

I miss you every day.

Contents

Dedication 7

Acknowledgments 10

Forward 11

Introduction 12

The Journey of Healing 18

Healing By Faith 21

How To Use This Book 27

Chapter One 33
    Re-mark – Renew 33

Chapter Two 51
    Re-mark – Emotions 51

Chapter Three 62

    Re-mark – Movies 62

Chapter Four 73

    Re-mark – Attitude 73

Chapter Five 84

    Re-mark – Regret 84

Chapter Six 93

    Re-mark – Keep Going 93

Epilogue: The X Factor 118

About the Author 123

One More Thing 124

Let's Stay Connected 125

Acknowledgments

Thank you to those that have walked alongside me on this journey. Your encouragement and prayers have strengthened and guided me to make *UNMASK: Stop Hiding, Start Living* become a reality.

Vicki McLachlan, Karen Maxwell, Kirsten Williams, Jelena Simpson, and Raquel Twigg, each of you, in your own way, has spoken into the purpose of this book and called it forth from within me.

Thank you, Catherine Mitchell, for jumpstarting me into writing this book with your gentle reminder, "Do it now, or you won't do it." Thank you for being obedient in making that call. Thank you for your encouragement, prayers, thinking, and creative partnership. You are greatly appreciated.

To Eric G. Reid, you called to the best in me as my editor and publisher. Thank you to you and to your incredible team at Skinny Brown Dog Media. You are all amazing.

To my husband Bill, whose support and love are unwavering and unconditional. Thank you for journeying this life with me, my darling.

Forward

Dear one,

As I read this book, I can hear Wendy sharing each story, each truth, each encouragement as if we were sitting together over coffee. As always, I am trying to take in her every word, trying to remember it all, because I know it is lived truth that comes from her heart and shared with such wisdom, grace and love.

Wendy's life is an inspiration, especially for those who have been impacted by trauma. She doesn't minimise or dismiss the challenges of living in this reality, but within these pages shares a practical roadmap towards courage and hope. For those who are tired of surviving behind a mask of pretence, Wendy offers practical steps that connect us to living authentically with hope, purpose and even joy!

I have had the privilege of hearing Wendy speak to groups of women on a number of occasions. Each time her words strike a chord that resonates within to bring deep reflection, connection and refreshment. This book reflects Wendy's gift of creating a safe space to drop the mask, to honestly see who we are, and then to find healing and hope not just for ourselves but for the relationships surrounding us. It fills me with faith to believe again that change is possible in my life, and hope in the pain and challenges of those I journey alongside.

After spending time with Wendy, I always come away feeling more accepting of who I am, with a renewed hope that healing and wholeness in life is possible, and a vision of my future which is purposeful and even exciting.

So, grab a journal and a pen, make yourself a hot drink and get ready… I truly hope that as you read these words you will see the light and discover the life you have been created for.

Jodi Traves

Pastor - Women and Community

Bridgeman Baptist Community Church

Introduction

> We can choose to turn our tears, our wounds and our traumas into courage, to walk with hope, and to walk into healing victory.

I lay in a stranger's bed in a stranger's house, holding my mum in my arms, trying to comfort her while pain, anguish, and heartbreak wracked her body. There was nothing I could say or do that would stop the pain, nothing that would take her away from what had just happened. No amount of alcohol or words would bring her comfort. I had just killed her husband, my dad.

When she finally fell asleep from the mixture of exhaustion and alcohol, I was allowed time to feel the full depth of pain and horror of what I had done. My brother and sisters were asleep in the next room. Each of us was in shock at a different level from the day's events. Together in the darkness of this strange house, I was trying to make sense of how an ordinary day ended up going so horribly wrong.

My aunt and uncle's house was so unfamiliar to me; we had visited maybe once before. This night I walked through the silent rooms crying, lost in grief and the darkness. From the far end of the house, my uncle called to me, "Come here, settle down. It's okay, it will be okay. Come lay down with me. Hush hush, child."

His words were a comfort to me in the emptiness of the night. My kind, loving, caring uncle asked me to let him cuddle me, assuring me that everything would be okay, to just let go and hush.

In the darkness at the back of this strange house, with tears still staining my face from killing my father, my uncle raped me. My screams to stop broke the night. My aunt rushed into the room, shouting at me, "What have you done?" as she dragged me into the hallway. Standing over me, this massive, angry figure made it clear that what had just happened was my fault. And that if I had any sense left in me, I should clean myself up, go back to bed, and tell no one.

Dazed and in shock, all I could feel was my body shaking and shivering with fear. I wasn't sure what had just happened—my body was in pain, my heart numb, and my mind could not make sense of any of this.

I was thirteen years old. I had no idea of what sex was and no understanding of rape, but I knew what had just happened was not kind, loving, or caring. And somehow, all of it was my fault.

I had ended up at my aunt and uncle's house because we had to flee our home earlier that day. That day my brother, sisters, and I spent the day playing in the snow while Mum and Dad drank the day away at the local pub. This day was unusual for so many reasons. On this day, instead of passing out in the gutter or being hauled off to the police station, our parents had walked home with us.

If there is one advantage of being a kid growing up in a small town, it's that if your parents pass out in the street, the police will step in, feed you, and care for you until your mum and dad sobered up, and you could take them home.

Even though he was a drunk, I loved my daddy. I would follow him everywhere; I was like his shadow. That day when we got home, dad went and lay on my bed, and I followed him.

Laying in my bed, my dad asked me to get his rifle, the one he used to go hunting. As I was always his obedient little girl, I raced to the front room to get the rifle. When I returned, he was lying in the bed, almost asleep. I handed him the rifle, not sure why he wanted it now, of all times. I had learned it was better not to question him, just do as I was told. Sitting up in the bed, looking me in the eyes, he said, "This is how you kill yourself."

BANG, in a flash, time collapsed back on itself. He was dead. He had put the barrel of the rifle in his mouth and pulled the trigger right in front of my eyes. Blood covered my bed. Blood ran down the walls of my room.

As my dad's body collapsed back into the bed, I ran screaming from the room. Grabbing my brother and sisters, I ran from the house and out into the road. The smell of gunpowder and blood chased us down the road and across the creek to the only place I could think of: to the house at the end of the road that belonged to my aunt and uncle. Bursting through the door, I screamed, "I killed Daddy!" With those words, my brother and sisters knew what had just happened and began screaming and crying.

I was thirteen years old. My father was dead because of me. My uncle had raped me. My aunt had shamed me into silence, and my mom was passed out, unable to protect me. I was beyond broken; I was shattered into a million pellets. My soul was cut open wide, and I struggled to breathe.

It would take years for me to look at the wounds from the trauma of that day. I can't call them scars yet, because scars come from healing, and I am still healing the parts I can safely face. Over the years, my wounds became infected with shame and guilt. Instead of working to heal, I hid behind the many masks that I created for my daily survival.

> **It's only when we find the courage to drop those masks and speak our story that true healing begins.**

I was in a play that was based on a story called the "Yay Yucky Man." This play revolved around the idea that we can get caught up wearing different-colored coats as camouflage in order to fit into different situations in life. When we believe that we are expected to be a certain type of person, we slip on the blue coat; the next situation might require us to wear a yellow coat or a purple coat until we wear so many of these different-colored coats—or masks as I call them—we no longer know who we really are.

These masks allow us to hide. They keep us from ever having to show the truth of what's inside of us, just like those colored coats. Even though I was just an actor in this play, I was perfectly cast for this play. I had been living behind masks for so long this role felt real to me.

In *Remarkable You*, my first book, I shared my deepest wounds. I put them out there for the world to see. I took off the mask and stood before the world and waited for their response. And I survived.

Writing and sharing *Remarkable You* was part of my journey to be fully free. I know how difficult exposing your wounds to others or even admitting them to yourself can be. Being vulnerable is the last thing any of us wants to do. We would rather keep our wounds and the trauma of our past concealed behind our masks. And being vulnerable and exposed to the world feels like certain death.

When we choose masks over the truth, we become trapped behind those masks. We lose any sense of the truth of who we are and what our purpose is. The only way to stop hiding and start living is to take off the mask and literally drop the mask to allow the re-marking to begin.

Unmask: Stop Hiding, Start Living was written because I had received so many requests from the readers of *Remarkable You* to give them a guide on how to discover their Remarkable and the hope within.

Unmask: Stop Hiding, Start Living will require that I go back into the events of my past to examine the events, traumas, shame, pain, and guilt that impacted my life and openly show you how I worked through the process of moving into healing. Not all wounds are healed, and because of that, I will exercise self-care. I know that I am not alone in these feelings and that you may carry equally deep wounds that you are in the process of healing. I encourage you to move at your own pace and exercise self-care. My journey is presented as a road map, not a challenge. Heal you as you need it.

In *Unmask: Stop Hiding, Start Living* I will be sharing my own experience of how I made my way through the pain and trauma to healing those deep wounds. This process allowed me to take off my many masks, to re-mark my life, and to know the real me living fully in my purpose and destiny.

If you have been wounded by trauma, pain, or the actions of others, or if you feel shame or guilt because of what has happened to you, now is the time to start to release those feelings. Maybe you feel less than, not enough, or inadequate because of the circumstances you have faced, or perhaps you carry so much baggage from your childhood of not being valued or cared for by your parents or abused by someone close to you. I see you and welcome you into this space. No matter what it is that has kept you locked behind a mask, living stuck in that wounded place, know that you are not alone and that I am grateful you chose to read *Unmask*. Congratulations on making this decision to start your journey of healing. Simply holding this book in your hand shows you are ready to no longer live in that wounded, masked place. Welcome to your journey of transformation.

Unmask is written to strengthen you on the journey to re-mark your life. This book is about taking action. I know that everything worthwhile is uphill, and uphill climbs are where healing begins. They are hard, but the view from the top is so worth the struggle. Getting started is the hardest part of the journey but also the most valuable part of your journey. And you have already started.

Determination and tenacity will be needed for this journey. And from my own experience, I know that you will never see the glory of the other side, the outcome you desire, unless you endure the uphill climb. Growth requires struggle. The more you are willing to struggle with your steps, the greater the outcome. Look at how a caterpillar struggles to come out of a chrysalis to become the most beautiful, remarkable butterfly it was always meant to be. So it will be with you.

On this journey, I will gently lead you to acknowledge the wounds that you carry. By seeing your wounds, you will use them to guide the action you need to take to become the remarkable you. In each chapter, I will lead you to take your next step, to acknowledge the hidden wounds, the destruction from those wounds, and the masks you wear that cover those unhealed wounds.

Healed wounds change our heart, our life, our perspective, our confidence, and our future. My prayer is that as you take the journey to heal through my words and encouragement, you will move from being stuck and disempowered to a place of empowerment, and the courage that I know is in you will rise boldly as you take each and every step on this journey. I call you on to re-mark your life in the truth of who you are.

The Journey of Healing

I am so mindfully aware that healing is not a straight line. Healing is not always a simple fix and not always a one-and-done event. Healing takes time, and it will look different for everyone. It requires incredible courage to overcome fear—the fear of what could happen if you acknowledge the wounds you are carrying, acknowledge the things that have happened to you. I know this fear can be so powerful it disempowers you, particularly around the process of healing. We become so paralyzed that we just settle and stay where we are, growing more and more familiar with that pain. We allow those masks to become who we are.

When we are wounded by trauma, by events, by circumstances, by life, the marks left on us by others, by society, we can feel that we must push the pain deep down inside and pop on our mask of all is well, and say we are okay. We tell ourselves we are okay without acknowledging the pain or allowing healing to begin. The world expects us just to stand up, brush ourselves off, and move on.

Our masks help us to look like the crowd, to blend in, and look like we have it all together. My mask was in the form of my clothes, the makeup I put on, and the bright lipstick that said to others that my life was full of joy, while inside, I was being consumed more and more by my wounds.

Maybe your mask is a loud, bold voice that gives you an appearance of confidence while you tremor inside. Maybe it's the timid voice you use to avoid being heard. Maybe your mask is anger or a stinky attitude

I covered my wounds with anger!

I covered my wounds with a stinky attitude!

I covered my wounds with excessive drinking!

I covered my wounds with hurtful words, actions, and attitude!

I covered my wounds with labels of importance!

I covered my wounds with people-pleasing!

I covered my wounds with self-sabotage!

I covered my wounds with suicidal ideation!

All covered in a good dose of fear!

Each of us wears a mask to cover the pain and fear that are our past at some point. The goal in life is to learn to live mask-free and happy.

As you start this journey, let me reassure you that you may think you are the only one that is fearful of the fix, but you are not. I was afraid for so long to even acknowledge that I needed healing. For way too long, I was not truly honest with myself, and I allowed my feelings of fear to dictate my truth. Honesty is essential on this journey of healing. I encourage you to take the time needed to go through the action steps provided in each chapter. Know that action steps require honesty with yourself to openly acknowledge the areas that need healing.

In chapter eighteen of *Remarkable You*, I shared the story of the ancient Greek marathon race. Let me quickly share this story with you again to set the scene for your journey ahead.

In the marathons of ancient Greece, a torch was handed to each runner at the starting line. To win, a runner had to cross the finish line with their torch still burning.

The marathon led through mountains and valleys. Doubtless, there were times when runners would pass each other. The lead runner's strength would fail, or their confidence might wane as their mind drifted to thoughts of not being good enough or worthy of finishing. A runner was not counted out if they went off course and had to retrace their steps. What determined the winner was not the style but the staying power to cross the finish line with the torch in hand still burning.

I can only imagine how each step required to run this race depended on the runner's ability to take able action, to find brave belief, and to choose courage over fear for the next step and the next. They had to stay focused, to find enduring strength, to discover staying power, to be empowered with hope, to look past fear, to be daring, and to run with a bold purpose to cross that finish line.

We are each called to run our best race and to cross the finish line with the torch burning in our hearts. Completing a full marathon is no easy feat. Even for seasoned runners to finish the race, they must set their minds to bravely face the road ahead, despite the pain and exhaustion, despite the fear, and choose the courage to keep going.

To run this race of healing and to finish well requires you to step up with that same great courage and bravery of the marathon runner and take the steps necessary to undergo the healing process as we unshackle ourselves from the wounds, rip away the masks, and re-mark our lives to live fully in the purpose we were created for.

Whether you realize it or not, I know that each of you already has the essential gifts you need for your journey. It's there inside each of you. It may be buried with the wounds. My remarkable friend, it's time to dig that courage up as we journey together if we intend to heal.

Healing By Faith

Throughout this book, there are glimpses of my faith. I am a person of faith. I share aspects of my faith because I can't share my story of healing without including my faith. Maybe you don't hold the same faith as me—that's okay. I am not asking you to share my faith. That's a choice. However, since this is my story of healing, my faith became a part of my healing and my truth. Please stay with me on this journey to the end, as I believe it will be the most worthwhile journey in your life. And for now, hold the idea of faith and God open, to be added as part of your healing in a way that fits you best.

My faith is built on a belief that each of us is God's handiwork. We were created uniquely; there is no one like you or me, and that is by God's design. We hold commonalities in our story, but we recognize our differences as well.

I can't be you, and you can't be me. I love the Scriptures because they reassure me of that fact, especially on the days that I feel like I can't go on. I remind myself that God already has a plan for me, just as He does for you. That plan is for each of us to live fully into the destiny and purpose we were created for.

> For we are God's handiwork, created in Christ Jesus to do good works, which God prepared in advance for us to do.
>
> **- EPHESIANS 2:10 NIV**

> We have become his poetry, a re-created people that will fulfill the destiny he has given each of us, for we are joined to Jesus, the Anointed One. Even before we were born, God planned in advance our destiny and the good works we would do to fulfill it!
>
> **- EPHESIANS 2:10 TPT**

God wrote a plan for your life, as He did for mine—a plan that's full of goodness and hope and a great future. His plan did not include the pain and trauma, but He did provide for the healing. He designed each of us to be able to heal and fulfill all the potential that He placed inside of us.

Every blow that has wounded and marked you was designed by the enemy of our souls to knock you down and take you out of the race. The enemy of your purpose has the desire to keep you from the very destiny of your life. Every wound will be used to try to deceive you into abandoning the purpose that God created you for from the day you were born.

How do you overcome the enemy of your purpose? How do you get the victory? Take it from someone who knows, someone who got up off my floor, said NO to suicide, and YES to life. The victory you seek comes when you stand up and take a step. No matter how many times you fall, you get up. Please, hear my voice, every small action you take to get up, to drag yourself forward, to grow and develop—no one can take that away from you.

The biggest victories are made one step at a time. I want to encourage you to keep going. With each brave, courageous step you defeat the enemy and move into healing and wholeness. Life will throw you a curve ball, and it will be frustrating and discouraging and make you feel like you're taking one step forward and two steps back but hold on.

Keep going, keep getting back up, and each time, you will feel stronger. On this journey, there will be so many battles won simply by outlasting the attacks. I know. I have been knocked down time and time again, and I am still here and thriving. We have no power to stop being knocked down, but we do have the power to make the choice to get back up and to discover the truth of who we are. Remember, staying power is often key!

My God is strong, and He wants you to be strong. He will reveal His strength to you so He can reveal His strength through you. Your story of overcoming will become your testimony, your story, when shared, will empower someone else to start the journey. There is power in our testimonies. Please know I am walking alongside you and praying for you.

The world counted me out, and there was a time I took myself out of this race. If I had listened to the world, to the lies of the enemy of my soul, I would have ended up like my parents. Know that today, as you are reading this, I am counting you in. I may not know your name, but hand on my heart, I know that there is a destiny just waiting for you to fulfill it.

I lost my ability to trust when the man that was supposed to love and care for me included me in his suicide. In that moment, my father abandoned me. I truly lost trust in everyone that day. So, when someone suggested I put my trust in an unknown father, they were asking me to do what seemed impossible. Maybe as you read this, you don't know who my Father God is. Don't fear. When I started my journey of healing, although I said yes to asking Jesus into my heart, I had no idea what that meant and what that would look like years later. But through my journey, very slowly, I finally realized that I have a Heavenly Father that I can trust, and I have now experienced Him over time acting in my life. Understand that He will wait for you to turn your trust to Him and to look to Him for your strength. He will demand nothing of you. You are in control of this relationship.

Isaiah 41:10 (AMP) says, "Do not fear [anything], for I am with you; Do not be afraid, for I am your God. I will strengthen you, be assured I will help you; I will certainly take hold of you with My righteous right hand [a hand of justice, of power, of victory, of salvation]." Even when I did not believe this Scripture, I found it to be true.

You were chosen. You were not an afterthought, no matter how you have been marked by the world or what the trauma and wounds have tried to make you believe. No matter the circumstances you grew up in, no matter what fears you face, no matter what words have been spoken over you, and no matter your age, you are God's chosen handiwork.

We are all so unique. Your journey will be different from anyone else's, but like all journeys, it will require one step that's the same as everyone else's. That is the first step of courage to want more for your life. That first step you take may be like mine, covered in tears and filled with fear, but once you take it, it's like breaking free of a sinking ship that is slowly pulling you into the depths of a dark ocean. My faith tells me the battle is not ours—it belongs to God. All we have to do is to take the next step forward, and He will lead us step by step, layer by layer, to unmask our wounds.

The enemy of our souls uses many tricks to fill us with fear. Sometimes his tricks are as simple as whispering in your ear, "You can't do it. You're not worthy. It's too hard. Oh, and what if you start this journey and you fail? You're an imposter, pretending to be someone you're not—what will people think of you?" That's he needs to say to stop you. You know what he says to you.

Please know, my dear friends, that as I am writing this book, I am praying that my words will be used as a catalyst for you to start your journey or, if you have started, to keep going. Know that I will be with you, each and every one of you, urging you on to step through the door past the fear as you say, "I see you, fear, but I'm going forward anyway!"

These words are important, so let me repeat them: "I see you, fear, and I hear your voice, BUT I choose to move forward and discover who I am."

Choose to step past, over, and around fear knowing that

> God has not given us a spirit of fear, but of power and of love and of a sound mind
>
> **- (2 TIMOTHY 1:7 NKJV).**

As I started my journey, my personal marathon, my torch was almost out. There was only a flicker of light left, but that little flicker of light was enough for me to know I could start. This starting point was a voice in my head that said, "We can choose to turn our tears, our wounds, and our traumas into courage, to walk with hope, and to walk into healing victory."

As you start this journey, your personal marathon, there are some key essentials to keep in mind:

1. This is a marathon and not a sprint; pace yourself.
2. Healing is not a straight line, and sometimes you will feel you are taking two steps forward and one step back.
3. You have not lost this race unless you stop.
4. Just because you may have traveled a distance down a road does not mean you can't turn around and choose a different route.
5. You are never too young or too old, and it's never too late to start.
6. Please don't let despair overtake your hope, as it can blind you to the promise of the future.
7. As Harriet Beecher Stowe said, "Never give up, for that is just the place and time when the tide will turn."

As you turn the page, be defiant and look fear in the eye and say, "I see you, but I choose to look past you." Then rip away your masks and take this journey to re-mark your life.

Please know I am praying for you.

Love,

Wendy

> Let this hope of a better future give you the strength and courage you need to work through the pain and hurt, not just to survive your past, BUT to live victoriously in the present.

How To Use This Book

At the end of every chapter, I will be encouraging you to dig deep and take the next few steps. These next steps will be essential on your journey.

You will find that each chapter will have its own **A, B, C's**.

You may choose to read the book completely and then come back and do the A, B, and C action steps. Or you may choose to read a chapter at a time, pause and complete A, B, and C action steps. You will know what's best for you. Let me say, though, that these action steps will empower you to unmask to re-mark your life. Action creates ownership—your action, not mine.

Let me set the scene with what A, B, and C is all about.

A

Action

Our futures are determined by our daily decisions, so each decision matters. Each choice matters. We all get to write our stories one page, one decision, and one step at a time. We never quite know what hangs in the balance of each decision we make. Each choice will take us further away or closer to a re-marked life. The things that become habitual are the things that shape our lives.

Nothing will change unless you take action to bring about that change. Believe me, I know this to be so very true. We need to take the action and be the change. Maybe you are like I was, waiting for someone else to take the action for me and to make the changes I so wanted and desperately needed in my life.

Change requires action on our part. Owning the action you take is fundamentally critical for this journey, and being accountable to yourself for those actions is essential. My friend, change is an inside job. It starts inside of us and plays out in the actions we take. It's called inside-out self-leadership.

B

Belief

Belief starts as an inside job.

- When I started my journey, I never thought I could do it simply because I had no belief in myself. I did not even believe that I was worthy of the journey.

- The opposite of belief is disbelief. If we lack belief in ourselves, we live in a place of disbelief that anything could be different or better and that we can be different. Belief will begin with the words you say to yourself.

- I started by looking at myself in the mirror with honest, hopeful eyes and telling myself, "I can do this." I told myself, "I will make this choice." In doing this, I found a small seed of belief to trust my words. This was one small action step—not a giant step, but one small step built on the seed of belief.

- I had lost everything, or so I thought. I could not go on in my own strength at that moment. My masks were gone. If God knew of my past and rescued me from a generational curse of suicide, then what would happen if I could have the belief that God would rescue me from the debilitating wounds I carried? I had two choices: find my bravery and choose to trust in this unknown God, or not. You have the same choices.

Belief in ourselves requires us to be brave. Being brave will look different for everyone.

- There are so many different words for brave: courageous, valiant, heroic, bold, daring, fearless, gutsy, determined. I could go on and on. Bravery, for me, is encapsulated in this quote:

"Bravery is not the absence of fear. Bravery is feeling the fear, the doubt, the insecurity, and deciding that something else is more important."

- MARK MANSON

- I will not tell you it will be easy, and there is no way around this truth. The healing process will require you to be honest with yourself, as I mentioned earlier.
- Being brave for me required me first to acknowledge that I was in a mess, and that life was not going to change unless I did.
- Being brave is also allowing the time and space to undertake the healing process and not expect it all to happen in one go.
- Your words matter. Acknowledging your brave and courageous self is important. Tell yourself, "I am brave, and I believe I can do this."

C

Choice

The power of choice means we have options.

- We each have the right and power to choose what we do. Remember that our stories are written one decision at a time.

- It took me until I was thirty-four years old to realize that I could choose to make a good decision and that the decisions I made would affect and play out not only in my life but in the lives of my children and grandchildren and the generations to come—just like my parents' decisions played out in my life. I have a choice about the legacy I want to leave.

- What took me much longer to understand is that I have to remake that choice every day. I must choose, every single day, to either look deeply at the wounds that are oozing into my life and impacting my decisions or ignore them.

- You have to start by understanding that you are worthy of making a good choice and that you can make those choices. You are worthy of the journey to full healing. It always starts with a choice.

Just like Belief requires us to be brave, Choice requires us to have courage.
I can't talk about courage without talking about that dreaded word: *fear!*

- Fear feels so powerful and so real, and the thought of facing the hidden, deep wounds can put us in flight-or-fight mode. Fear is so real in someone who is broken. I know I have felt many, many times the heart palpitations, the taste in my mouth, and the panic that comes with fear.

- Please hear my heart: There is no guilt or shame in feeling fear. The steps of courage you take when that fear comes are what count.
- What is courage? Look at this description and see if it resonates with you as it did with me:

Courage is like a door inside each of us. It's a door with a knob only on the inside. A door that only we can open for ourselves. Others can cheer us on, but they can't open the door to take the steps we need to take on the journey. Choosing the courage to open the door is the first step of courage we can take.

What I want you to know is that, yes, fear is real, but the courage and bravery in you are also real. You have the courage to look fear in the face and say, "I see you," but...

I choose to move forward anyway!

I choose to move past you!

I choose to open the door to courage.

I choose to step through the door of courage.

These truths, these statements of affirmation, are tools that you will create for yourself on this journey of healing. They will be like weapons in your arsenal that you use to speak your truth across your life.

In *Remarkable You*, I shared "A Journey to Discover Hope." Hope is very powerful and necessary, but it is not enough on its own. Hope is what we feel in our heart, but it needs to partner with action. Action is what makes the difference.

As you come with me on this journey to unmask and re-mark your life, you will find a BIG focus on the actions required to bring about change and transformation. I know from my experience of abuse, alcoholism, rape, and suicide that to heal the wounds and toxicity of these wounds, I needed to act. I needed to take action that no one else could take for me.

This is my formula for change:

> **Action + Belief + Choice = Re-Mark = TRANSFORMATION**

This quote speaks to the heart of this:

> Hope has two beautiful daughters; their names are Anger and Courage. Anger at the way things are, and Courage to see that they do not remain as they are.
>
> **- AUGUSTINE OF HIPPO**

I was angry for way too long without taking the action that only I could take for change. Somehow along the way, on my marathon journey, courage started by finding a seed of hope that life could be different. The day I took that first step of courage by not taking my life, the seed of who I am becoming now, I started to focus on my self-talk and not allow my emotions to control me. I focused on my attitude and told myself that I could do this, that I could keep opening the door of courage, and that no one could open it for me.

I knew in my soul that I needed to take the action, to step past fear—and past failure, shame, guilt, and all the other nasty little bits of baggage in my life—and be courageous. It's an inside job, and it's there inside each of us; sometimes we just must dig deep to dig it up. I know you can do the same!

Let the journey begin...

Chapter One

Re-mark – Renew

Healing takes courage, and we all have courage, even if we have to dig a little to find it.

- TORI AMOS

As we begin this journey, I will be nothing but honest with you. This journey will be hard and scary. Your inner voice of fear may be saying, *Stop now*. Your trust in me is a gift I treasure and will honor on this journey together. I know that there is a spirit of bravery in you. You can do this. As you journey through these pages and the A, B, and C portions, please take your time and be kind to yourself. If at any stage you feel unsafe or old triggers are being activated, please, please seek the help and support you need. This is a journey, not a race.

Why do I use the word re-mark? Because when we are born, each of us has our very own unique markings, our fingerprints. These fingerprints identify us and declare who we are, even in legal terms. These fingerprints tell the world there is no one like us. You were created with a unique purpose and destiny. This divine purpose and destiny are a mark placed on you long before your birth, long before the world met you and began to place its marking on your life.

From the moment we enter the world, we become marked by our circumstances—our family of origin, our culture, our upbringing, and our social and economic status. All these circumstances mark our lives in some way. Some markings are good, but as in my case and like many other women across the world, some of us have been marked by darkness and trauma. These marks are dark and so deep that they create wounds that can take a lifetime to heal.

As we grow and change, our fingerprints remain the same, and our physical identity at the core will remain the same except for the marks added by time and life. The truth of who we are gets lost and buried beneath the marks, the wounds of life.

The experiences of our life make us who we are. We lose sight of who we were born to be. Our dreams and purpose get buried by the damage of the wounds. These marks come in many sizes, shapes, and forms. They can be caused by words spoken over us, actions of others against us, and yes, even our own words and actions.

> **These wounds become the filters for our life.**

The words spoken over me became how I saw myself. I accepted others' beliefs that I was not worthy of love, care, acceptance, or life itself. These wounds became so deep that, over time, I treated myself exactly like others did. Broken, damaged, and unworthy was the filter I saw everything through. What others had marked me as had become a self-filling prophecy!

Each of us carries wounds, and the same experience will mark each of us differently. As I share my experiences, it is not for comparison purposes but simply to share. The experiences that created your wounds may have started in childhood, like mine. I lived in a home where I was constantly told I was no good and that I didn't have worth. A home filled with alcoholic abuse, rape, and suicide was simply the start.

The wounds of childhood may cause us to withdraw, cover-up, or become aggressive. We play out the wounds and our pain in games and make-believe. As we become teenagers and adults, we add alcohol, drugs, self-loathing, and self-sabotage to our coping mechanisms—all in the hopes of covering the wound and dulling the oozing pain. We battle every moment to hide and cover up the truth of how we have been marked, afraid to allow others to see who we really are. We find ourselves trapped behind our many masks, carefully choosing different masks with different people until we end up not even knowing who the real "me" is.

Your collection of wounds may have started for you as a teenager, young adult, adult, or even recently. It does not matter when the wounds began. They are real and will have the same effect. We are wounded at some level, we all bleed, and we all try to cover the wounds. We try a thousand different ways to hide them from the world and from ourselves. But we are marked with these wounds, and they can only be hidden for so long before they start to infect our lives.

Some wounds will be slight and heal without much intervention; but it's those deep wounds—the ones we hide deep inside while telling ourselves and those around us that we're okay—that are oozing away, seeping into our hearts and minds, weeping their toxic evil into our lives.

The shame and guilt I carried from handing my dad the gun became my deepest belief that I was responsible for his death. The guilt, shame, and sense of responsibility for someone else's choice attached to me. On that day, any joy that I had hoped to have in life was stolen from me. The trauma that created those wounds was deep, and it deepened and multiplied that night when I was raped. That day I was marked deeply by the actions of others. People I'd thought I could trust and who were meant to love and care for me instead cut into the very core of who I was and left marks that I would carry well into my adulthood.

Instead of seeking healing for these wounds, I fed them. I kept them open, infecting them over and over with my shame, guilt, and sense of unworthiness. I lived life through the filter that what had happened was my fault, that I had somehow caused others to treat me that way. This belief in my value impacted everything I did. These wounds marked me in a way that left me feeling like my life was hopeless and I was fated to live a life like my parents. I identify with shame and guilt. I allowed these feelings to diminish me and determine who I was and who I wasn't. Shame, guilt, and a sense of unworthiness dictated what I did and who I was becoming.

As I think of these wounds and the effort, I took to hide them, a picture of an octopus comes to mind. Did you know that a Blue-ringed octopus spends most of its life hiding in crevices displaying camouflage patterns? Like all octopuses, they can squeeze into crevices much smaller than themselves. This, along with piling up rocks outside the entrance to their hiding spot, helps safeguard the octopus from predators. Just like the Blue-ringed octopus, I hid and camouflaged myself from the world. Like the octopus, if I was provoked, I would quickly change disguises and withdraw deeper into my hiding place. Those of us hiding ourselves and our wounds from the world have learned how to shut down our feelings and quickly shift into our "I'm ok" camouflage.

My dear friend, unless we deal with the camouflaged wounds we carry, they will eventually kill our hope, our dreams, and our very future, all while playing havoc on our emotions and our mindset and, yes, sadly, our physical health too.

What happens is over time we become one with the wounds. Everything we see and do is through the filter of those wounds. We become known to ourselves and others only by our wounds. We become perpetual victims of our wounds. These wounds ooze into our thoughts and play out in our actions and our self-talk. Our unhealed wounds can take on many different shapes in our lives and remain hidden by the masks we wear.

In my day-to-day life, no one, absolutely no one, would have known about the wounds hidden inside of me. I became good at camouflaging what was inside of me. Those wounds were well camouflaged and hidden in the dark places and crevices of my soul. Those wounds that were only known to me would sneak out and remind me they were there when I was alone. It was then the quiet voices whispered in my head, reminding me that I am not worthy, that I am broken and spoiled and should be ashamed of myself.

The thoughts *I am worthless, I am pathetic, I am undeserving, I am not enough, I am unlovable, I am ugly, I am rejected, I am a disgrace, I am a fake*, ring over and over in our heads. We create our own personalized labels—labels thick and deep that keep the wounds open. We live those labels, and just like wounds that don't heal, those words and labels ooze out everywhere in our lives. And yes—excuse the vivid picture—those wounds can even become like poison as they get into our whole system, invading every area of our lives and paralyzing us from moving forward in any way.

From my experience and the experiences shared with me by those I have worked with, that poison runs deep. These wounds lay camouflaged to the world, slowly infecting all areas of our lives with their poison. We learn to live more and more in brokenness, becoming one with that wound, although not willingly. And, sadly, we're often unable to break free on our own because we have become so trapped in the tentacles of those wounds. We stop knowing how to believe we have the strength to break free. The thought of trying to face the healing process and the fear that freedom brings feels worse than living with our wounds. So, we go on day after day masked, hiding, not really living.

That is where I was not so long ago. Trapped, filled with so much poison and pain, I was preparing to take my own life. Months before, I had agreed to follow Jesus. I dutifully said the words I was told to say, thinking that would be enough for me to break free and be healed.

I worried that if anyone knew who I was underneath my churchgoer mask, my real story, they would not accept me even in the church. God would not even accept me. I needed to look like I had it all together. I need to remain self-contained and in control. At this point in my life, I was working overtime to control my life and the beliefs of others. Can you relate to this? Well, this good churchgoer was an enormous bogus story, living a lie from the pit of hell.

Here I was, autonomous and controlling, and why wouldn't I be after everything that happened to me? One of the many things I have learned on my journey to healing and hope is that

> **God can't work with someone unwilling to make room for others in their life.**

God will up the ante with the self-governing people. He wants us to be healed of these life-debilitating wounds, and for that to happen fully, we need to be prepared:

- to acknowledge that we are wounded;
- to acknowledge courageously that for change to happen, a transformation has to be from within;
- to acknowledge that we need the healing process;
- to trust and be trusting on God; and
- to ask God to lead us through the healing process step by step.

I wonder if you are currently like I was. I hid these wounds so well, even from my family and those closest to me, that people who saw me as confident and successful did not know how empty I was. Occasionally they would see me behave in a way that did not match the mask I was wearing; but for the most part, I had gotten really good at tucking everything dark and painful behind my mask of "everything is ok." I was very self-contained. I wore different masks depending on who I was with. I had my labels of success, which I wore very proudly, thinking they would make me look worthy and acceptable.

We all have the courage and ability to deal with the wounds of the past. For me, I was forced to tap into my courage to deal with the past wounds when my career was taken away without warning. You see, it was easy for me to put on the successful career woman mask each day. It made me look important and purposeful. Wearing that mask of my job title made me worthy, made me someone, and made me presentable to the world. Then suddenly, it was ripped away, and there was nothing left of me. Without that label, I was nothing. No one would respect me, and I was again worthless.

Alone at home, I sat on the floor with my wounds exposed and oozing everywhere, sobbing uncontrollably, feeling that it was all gone, my life was over, and there was nothing left. What would I do? There was no hope. What was left for me? Every emotion, every hurt, every pain told me, "End it. Take your life. Be done with it."

Deep inside of me, I could feel this tiny, almost unrecognizable speck of courage speaking out, saying, "Don't! Stop! Take the next step forward, get up, just try—please." What step? What would I do? How could I get up from this? The only choice I knew to make was to reach out my hand to God. Whether He was real or not, I would know soon enough. Life or death, that was the power of this choice.

I started my journey of healing from such a low point in my life—literally from the floor that day. I courageously made the choice to fight on, not to give up, to find a way forward, to get up. I now know that the first step of courage is always the hardest but the most meaningful. My first step was my step into life. Each step after that required me to listen to that voice of courage inside of me. The more I listened for courage, the more I found it, step by step, moment by moment.

The choice I made that day and the choices I continue to make enable me to battle the giants I have faced, to un-mask the guilt and shame, and take the healing journey. Part of my healing is sharing my story. It's remarkable the power of sharing our stories. Sharing who we are is so life-changing and requires tapping into that courage that is in each of us.

I remember making the decision to write my story in what became my first book, *Remarkable You*. I remember the level of fear and freedom I felt as my family read the rough draft. For the first time, they would know who I really was and see the ugly, broken, wounded mess I was inside. When each family member read my story, I held my breath, waiting to hear them say aloud the words that for so long I had told myself: "You're not worthy of love," "You don't deserve happiness," and "You should be ashamed of yourself."

However, tapping into that last ounce of courage and telling my story allowed me to experience the love of family fully. There were questions, but there was also love. Their love helped heal those wounds and free me to discover my new story.

A friend once told me, "If you don't deal with your demons (the marks/wounds), they go into the basement of your soul and lift weights." I so identify with this statement.

Weightlifters lift weights to gain strength. The wounds of past traumas and hurts become evil demons in your deepest darkest parts, getting stronger and stronger when you don't speak about them. They grow stronger and take over more and more of your life.

That stuff that has marked and penetrated your life doesn't simply go away if ignored. It doesn't fix itself. Instead, those demons hide out and grow stronger in that basement of your soul, just waiting and waiting until the right moment to rear their ugly heads and cripple you with fear and shame.

That's what happened the day I lost my job. Those old demons of shame, guilt, humiliation, and worthlessness were just waiting to step right up and lead me to the path of suicide.

What's in our hearts, surfaces in our thoughts, our beliefs, and our words and plays out in our actions. That moment when the mask I wore in the form of my job title was ripped from me, and my wounds were allowed to burst open and lay bare before everyone, I was broken. The loss and pain were so great I thought the only way out was to take my life as my mother and father had.

As Andy Stanley says, "Your legacy, your mark, your fingerprints on the future are determined by the decisions you make." This was a "decision moment" for me, a moment that would echo out from me and into my family. I stood at a defining crossroad moment dependent on me risking trusting one more time. If I could trust again, it would change my life and truly enable me to see that I could start over. That one moment of trust, that moment of making a courageous choice to allow the healing of my wounds and the re-marking of my life, would break generations of trauma.

No longer was it a choice to give up or go on. I had to take the next step by getting up off the floor and trusting I was worthy of living. Are you at a crossroad moment in your life, a moment of choice? If so, I pray my words will enable you to stand up and take the next step on this journey.

When we are broken, we often live an exterior life focused on maintaining the perfect exterior, not healing the wounds hidden deep on the inside. A perfectly compartmentalized life allows us to function at the level of worldly acceptance. This is dangerous because your life may look great to outsiders, but the hidden life is still there, doing its damage and destruction.

The hiding of my pain started for me as a little child in the early years of school, when I was told I was dirty and that I was not good enough to hang around with the other kids. During the long hours of loneliness, I would sit in the gutter with my brother and sisters outside the pub, waiting for our parents.

I knew I was different. I knew I was not good enough. I had been told often enough by my teachers and by the kids at school that I was not part of their class, even if I did not fully understand what that meant. I was already struggling to understand the life and circumstances I was in, often pretending to be someone else. When my dad took me deeper into the darkness that was surrounding his life and then my uncle raped me, I began to believe that I really was the cause of all the pain and darkness my life held.

To begin to move away from the path of suicide, I had to sit and unpack all those feelings and find my truth. I had to understand that even though bad, unthinkable stuff does happen, I was not bad. I was not the cause of the dark and evil in the world. I could make a choice to have a different life, a life that changed generational history and create the legacy that I wanted to leave. For this shift to happen, I needed the light of the truth to show me the way out.

As I have told you, the journey to un-mask and stop hiding and start living *starts* with a step.

The first step is to acknowledge the wounds and name them. This requires us to go back to the moment where it all started and, at an emotional level, reexperience fully what happened, acknowledge that what happened, and speak out loud that how we felt was real, regardless of what others said. Only then can we take the actions to begin to work on forgiving the perpetrator and forgiving ourselves.

As part of my healing process, I spent a lot of time writing out those stories of trauma and pain and identifying what the truth of the story was and what my feelings were in the moment and after. When I was able to really look at what happened and stop blaming myself, I was able to choose to believe the truth that I am worthy of life, that I matter, and that I am beautifully and wonderfully made. My belief was shaky in the beginning, but I decided to own this truth. Yes, I did have to dig deep into my braver self to hold onto this belief. I realized that my story did not need to be set in stone. Who I was could change, and the truth of who I was did not come from the wounds I carried but from who I was before I entered the world.

Let me explain. The emotions attached to our wounds will not tell us the truth about who we are. They instead try to lead us to believe that we are a permanent victim of those wounds. It's only as we extract the truth of who we are from the emotions and lies of those events that we un-mask and find out our truth.

In the examples I have shared about my father and uncle, I believed the lies that I was responsible for my father's death and the rape by my uncle. The emotions attached to these two wounds that echoed each other in their cruelty were so big, strong, and believable that they empowered the truth of being unworthy of love and being responsible for both events. I became trapped in this false narrative, resulting in me living every moment in that victim space.

As I un-masked these wounds, it was so important for me to reframe the narrative that I was telling myself. My father made a choice that I had no control or understanding of. I was a little girl that loved and obeyed her dad. I did not invite the rape by my uncle. I was an innocent child that was taken advantage of by a broken adult I trusted but who meant only to fulfill his needs.

It's so important, dear ones, to reframe the stories we tell ourselves. We have the power to choose what we believe about ourselves, and we have the power to act on what we believe. The actions we take change the ownership we take.

To enable my journey of healing and change, I created some affirmations that I wrote and said out loud as often as I needed. I call them my "choose to know" statements. I encourage you to write your own affirmations and keep adding to them as you go.

- I choose to know that I am able.
- I choose to know that I have brave belief.
- I choose to know that I have the courage to make better choices.
- I choose to know that I am worthy of a different life.
- I choose to know that despite my circumstance, my past, and my age, I decide my future.
- I choose to know that if I hang onto my marks, my labels, my wounds, and my past memories, I will miss out on the great future, the one that I was created to live out.
- I choose to know that if I let go of the past, my hands will be free to hold all the good things, all the good gifts that God has for me.
- I choose to let my defences down and trust this unknown God.

Join me on the journey to unmask your life.

Let the hope of a better future give you the strength and courage you need to act and work through the pain and hurt not just to survive but to live victoriously in the present.

> The Lord will fight for you, and the victory will come with each and every step you take forward.

Psalm 147:3 assures us that the Lord "heals the broken-hearted and binds up their wounds" and that "He heals the wounds of every shattered heart." Our past does not dictate our future. This lesson is so important to keep in the front of our hearts on this journey of re-marking.

Up the Hill We Go

After acknowledging you are wounded and ready to heal, you must own your self-leadership. Learning to lead ourselves well on this journey is imperative. No one else can do this for us. This is a journey that we must lead ourselves on. It is ok and important to seek counseling and support if the wounds are so damaging that you can't work through them on your own. That decision is yours alone to make and act on. It's your action that counts. No one is going to give you back control of your life; you need to earn back control through your actions.

What is self-leadership? It's being accountable to yourself, telling yourself the truth, and no longer making excuses. It's about ownership. When we make excuses, we forfeit the ability to change the story and change ourselves.

> **Excuses will keep you stuck where you are.**

It's okay if you are scared and feel that fear rising in your throat, the fear that is almost a palpable taste. Remember, we look fear eye-to-eye and say, "I see you, but I choose to move forward!" I was scared and only able to take one small step towards acknowledging that I needed healing. Thankfully, small steps over time lead to great change.

A B C

Call to Action – Renew

At the end of each chapter, I will be asking you to take some time to reflect on the chapter. I will be prompting you with questions and encouraging you to use a journal to record your answers. There is great power in journaling.

With journaling, you will find three primary benefits. The first is clarity. The process of putting things on paper forces us to be precise. It's the way we take our thoughts captive.

The second benefit is memory. According to neuropsychologists, writing things down has a "generation effect." We develop better memory for the things we've written down than for things we read.

Third, documenting your journey will help you with the healing process.

Using these ABCs as you journal:

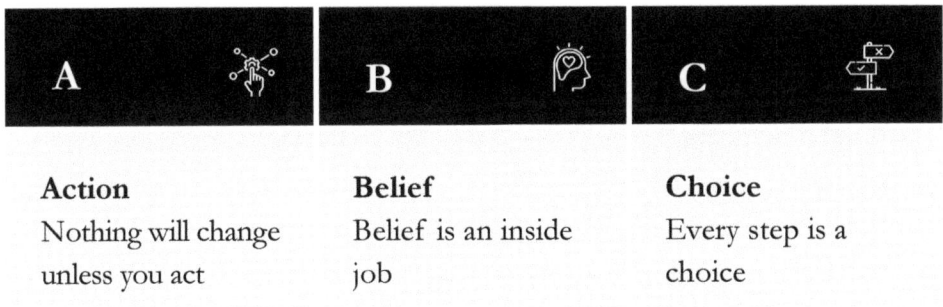

Action
Nothing will change unless you act

Belief
Belief is an inside job

Choice
Every step is a choice

Journal Prompt One

A
Action

If we want life to be different, learning to identify what's going on within our hearts and minds is critical.

Being honest with yourself is needed on this journey. That honesty starts now. No one will know what you write, and only you will know if you are truly honest with yourself during this process. No one else will read your answers but you. But the result you achieve will be directly proportional to the level of honesty you commit to.

1. Start writing out your story and identify the trauma, the wounds that have marked you and that are impeding you from living fully in the life you hope to live.

2. What are the life- and joy-stealers in your life? Can you identify how they show up? Do they look like guilt, shame, controlling behaviors, worthlessness, domestic violence, or humiliation?

Please don't rush this process. Take your time to write out the wounds you carry slowly but bravely, the ones you know affect you each day. Start with just one wound and work through how it has impacted your life, and when you're ready, look at the next one. I started with my dad's suicide and then worked on being raped by my uncle. It took me quite a lot of journaling to fully explore that day and who I thought I was.

Journal Prompt Two

B
Belief

When we carry deep wounds, we can get caught up in blame mode. I was blaming everyone and everything for the mess my life was in. Breaking through blame is where you need that brave belief.

I truly don't know any way forward without forgiveness, but that is the truth. My life would have been dire if I had not taken the step of this unfair burden called forgiveness. I would have spent my life as a victim and ended up dead by suicide had I not traded fairness for forgiveness.

> **Sometimes we need to trade fairness for forgiveness and freedom**

I understand that it does not seem fair that you should have to forgive; but the fact is, to break free from being a victim you have to forgive.

What is forgiveness? Wikipedia defines forgiveness as "the intentional and voluntary process by which one who may initially feel victimized undergoes a change in feelings and attitude regarding a given offense and overcomes negative emotions such as resentment and vengeance" (however justified it might be). Forgiveness is a voluntary decision, not a feeling. If we go by our feelings, then forgiveness may not be possible.

Don't try to work through the act of forgiveness all at once.

From what you have identified in **A**:

1. Who do you need to forgive?
2. Where do you need to forgive yourself?

Unforgiveness keeps us in an excuse mood, always blaming someone else.

If your desire is to unmask and stop hiding and start living your life for the better, then forgiveness is a necessary step.

I am encouraging you to forgive through the process of this journey. Forgiveness will be an ongoing process.

Take the time you need to forgive each person who has harmed you. Understand that forgiveness does not mean you need to bring these people into your life again. It does mean freeing yourself from them.

Forgiveness does not have to occur face-to-face; it can be written in your journal, or if you are a person of faith, it can be in the form of a prayer. This forgiveness is for you, not them. This forgiveness is for your healing, not theirs.

You can use words like "I choose not to blame or hold the actions of (name) against him/her," or "Where I have felt betrayed by (name), I forgive them."

Also, remember that you will need to forgive yourself. Forgive yourself for holding onto the wound. Tell yourself, "I choose to no longer hold on to (circumstance) with (name). Where I have carried (shame, guilt, name), I forgive myself."

For me, I needed to pray and ask the Lord to guide me on the journey of forgiveness of my father, my uncle, my mother, and most importantly myself.

When forgiveness is not complete, it begins to break down, bitterness takes hold, and our wounds are reinfected.

> Forgiveness starts here. Forgiveness liberates the soul, it removes fear, that is why it is such a powerful weapon. The past is the past; we look to the future
>
> – NELSON MANDALA

Journal Prompt Three

C
Choice

You have identified a few wounds, and you have taken the time to think about forgiveness and maybe even started the forgiveness process. Now it is time to move into some very practical steps you can take to leave those lies and wounds in the past.

Use your journal to reframe the stories you have written out in **A**.

It's time to identify what is truth and what are emotions.

> **Our emotions don't always tell us the truth.**

In the next chapter, I will write more about emotions, but for now, just take a moment to see if you can determine the difference. What are your emotions as you think back to the time when those wounds first appeared? Name them. Can you separate the emotion from the truth of the event? Were you really to blame, or were you told to feel shame when the truth was you were innocent and frightened? Often, we record our stories of trauma based on how we are supposed to feel versus how we really feel.

1. Review what you have written and look at it from a different perspective. Read what you have written carefully. Are the feelings you have written truly how you felt, or do they reflect how you thought you should feel? Do the feelings support the truth or the lie you have become trapped within? What are your facts?

2. Now, looking at yourself in those events, do you see your courage—the courage to survive, the courage to try to speak up before being shut down? It may be hard to see, but hiding in the darkness of my uncle's house after being raped, I had the courage to keep breathing and not give up. Highlight your moments of courage and write them out.

To see differently, this is how the unmasking begins. This is courage in action.

Life is full of emotional, spiritual, and mental pain to varying degrees. However, we get to decide to take the easy way out or work through the pain and grow into healing.

My prayer is that you will walk through the pain and into the remarkable you that you were born to be.

Chapter Two

Re-mark – Emotions

> If you don't deal with your demons (the marks/wounds) they go into the basement of your soul and lift weights just waiting for the opportunity to pounce when you least expect it and boom—they have taken control of your emotions and actions.

If you don't deal with your demons (the marks/wounds) they go into the basement of your soul and lift weights just waiting for the opportunity to pounce when you least expect it and boom—they have taken control of your emotions and actions.

The way that we get to know the demons in the basement is by paying attention to the emotions that fight for control of our moods and our behaviors. Our demons are those thoughts and beliefs that compete for control of our thoughts, words, and actions, those destructive emotions that are hidden behind our mask.

One dictionary defines emotion as "a strong feeling deriving from one's circumstances, mood, or relationships with others." What that definition fails to tell us is how our emotions can affect all that we do.

"Motions are the precursors of emotions," according to M. Asch. This means that the movement or waves of our emotions is a rising indicator that something is about to happen.

Growing an awareness of your emotions starts by understanding the role they play in your life and the influence they hold over your thoughts, actions, and internal and external language. Maybe you can't change all your emotions at once, but you can start to change the most destructive ones through your actions.

Research suggests that how we see our feelings and emotions, whether they are good or bad, controllable or uncontrollable, will affect us in important ways. Emotions will determine our outlook on life. What we empower will devour us. When we empower our good, positive emotions, we see the joy in the moments of life around us, and we feel those moments of happiness. When we empower our bad or negative emotions, they stop us from thinking in a rational way. They cloud our true assessment of what's happening and what we feel, making us see and remember only what we want to see and remember.

Our emotions are not always bad or good on their own. Rather, you can modify your emotions when they are not generating behaviors, actions, or internal and external language that are beneficial to you.

We honor our emotions by acknowledging them, simply saying, "I feel such anger rising within me." Then, by naming the emotion, we can change it. Consider the *why* of what you feel, the truth of the moment. Ask yourself, "Is this situation worthy of this anger and rage? What is the truth of this moment?" Taking the time to look deeper into the moment and not just react to every emotion that comes at you is so important on this journey. I know that, for me, my emotions ruled my life. How could I trust my ability to find truth when I was told to feel shame instead of pain, terror, and brokenness?

The role emotions play out in our lives is not a new thing. This great quote from Vincent Van Gogh from way back in 1889 says it clearly:

> Let's not forget that the little emotions are the great captains of our lives, and we obey them without realizing it.

On your marathon journey to unmask and live your life, you certainly wouldn't want those little demons in the basement driving your decisions.

Jonatan Martensson said, "Feelings are much like waves. We can't stop them from coming, but we can choose which ones to surf." During this journey of healing, I became aware of how my emotions played out in my daily decisions, actions, and behavior. I started to realize how those demons dictated everything, even those thoughts on suicide. I was stuck so deep in the muck and mire of my emotions and the patterns I had created in my mind of hopelessness that I saw no way to change or move forward. I was surfing every single emotion that came at me—surfing and drowning in them as I felt those feelings crash in on me.

One day at Dudley Beach in Newcastle, Australia, the water was rough and choppy, with loads of waves crashing at the shore. I loved being in the water, so I thought I would be fine to go in for a swim.

Just like the emotional waves that come at us, those waves on that day came at me thick and fast. I was dumped and dragged under the surface and fought to get back on top of the wave. Choking and bracing for the next wave, I began to panic. Could I make it back to the surface again, or was I going to go under, never to be seen again as my children watched me from the shore? Lost beneath the wave, unable to determine which direction to swim, I heard those demons start. They mocked me for trying, teasing me that I would never make it safely back to shore, and telling me it would be better just to give up. Finally, someone grabbed my arm from above. It was in that moment that I had the courage to hush the demons and swim. Safely on shore, I thanked my rescuer and my voice of courage.

When those dark demon emotions start to take over, they will feel like those waves that day at the beach, crashing all around you, leaving you with a sense of not being able to make it out alive.

Our emotions don't always tell us the truth about our situation. Let me begin by explaining what I mean. As you begin to lead yourself well and grow in your awareness and understanding of how your emotions can affect all that you do, you will see how emotions can color everything. Allowing emotions to lead can alter your perspective and your ability to handle adversity, failure, criticism, change, and pressure. Emotions will also dictate the masks you put on.

We use masks to enable us to blend into the crowd, move through the world undetected, and be seen as acceptable and unbroken. We put them on to look like we have it all together, that we are enough. We wear our masks to avoid the judgment of our truth. Masks can allow you to look like an altogether mother and a successful businesswoman, an altogether human. But wearing a mask can wear us out, so that when we take it off, our truth surfaces and the demons wake up to overtake us, like those waves that day on Dudley Beach. Maybe those waves show up in the form of anger, uncontrolled yelling, drinking, and disappearing to get through the next few hours until we can put on our mask again.

I have seen firsthand how unhealed wounds like guilt and shame lead to destructive, unhealthy behaviors that create a cycle of more guilt, more shame, and more self-loathing. The emotional demons love to pounce at an opportunity to take us on a cyclone-level wave of flashbacks and emotions that dump us and drag us down again and again.

You may not be as lucky as I was that day and have a rescuer pull you to the surface. That is why self-leadership is essential. Self-leadership is the self-management of those emotional waves. It enables you to take control of those tsunamis of emotions and behaviors that try to keep you from becoming who you were called to be. And it gives you the courage and ability to lead yourself to a safe place. Understand that sometimes that safe place is not the final destination in your journey but simply a place to catch your breath, reset your bearings, and prepare your next best step.

Not all emotions we experience in life are bad. Our souls need to experience emotions of happiness, excitement, joy, hope, and inspiration. It's vital we create experiences that produce these emotions for us. Such emotions can lead us to act in positive, life- and self-affirming ways that make us comfortable to go maskless into the world.

There is a great proverb to remind us that what's inside of us can affect what we do:

> Pay attention to the welfare of your innermost being, for from there flows the wellspring of life.
>
> **(PROVERBS 4:23 TPT)**

The day my job title mask was ripped away, all those little hidden wounds rose up and took control.

You see, I had worked my way up in government into a senior position. My mistake was that I had a belief that my job title, and my important role, made me who I was, and I allowed it to become my self-worth. I had connected all of who I was to the job, all the while neglecting to heal those deepest wounds.

Now, I was unmasked and left only with my wounds and all the emotions that had been hiding in the darkness of my soul. Before we continue, let me briefly share how my unmasking occurred, to give you a sense of how out of control we are in our unmasking. You see, false allegations were made to the Crime and Misconduct Commission about me. While the investigation was conducted, I was put on administrative leave. My label of importance was ripped away in a moment, and I was powerless to stop it from happening. My very important job and very important job holder mask was gone. I was now a senior-level employee under a government misconduct investigation. A big fall.

The day following my fall, I sat on the floor of our home. My husband had gone to work. The children were grown and gone. Alone in our home, I sat on the living room floor, planning my suicide. As far as I was concerned, everything that made me who I was had disappeared. There was nothing left. I had no value. No worth to my family. There was no need for me live.

My emotions of fear, anger, and failure were real at that moment, but they weren't telling me the truth about who I am and my current situation. As I sat there thinking of my plan to take my life, my thoughts raced back to being in that room with my dad as he took his life and how it wounded me. Then my thoughts leaped to my mum's suicide and her many poor life choices. My dad and my mother had made choices without thinking about the wounds those choices would leave on me, my sisters, and my brother. Both could not see past their pain. If I took my life, what would I be doing to my husband and children?

Seeing past my pain, I could start to see the facts. I could see past the overwhelming feelings and emotions.

As I sat there on the floor, alone, I started to think of what was true. My dad made the decision to get me to hand him his rifle; he pulled the trigger, not me. I didn't kill him. Yet somehow, I had chosen to carry the weight of responsibility for over thirty years.

My uncle raped me. The feelings of shame and guilt belonged to my aunt and uncle, not me. My mum chose to end her life, not me. The investigation was the result of someone else's lie, not truth. These were the facts. The pain felt deeply real at that moment. To survive this moment of overwhelming emotions, I needed to focus on the facts and not be taken over by my feelings. I was in a dark battle for my life—a dark battle with a voice that promised me all the torment and pain could end.

I had worn so many masks in my life. Each mask I wore, thinking it was protecting me from the feelings of those events, had really prevented me from seeing the facts of the trauma, including my true feelings and emotions, and who was actually responsible for what had happened. My masks prevented me from healing.

Surely my life was of greater value than these dark emotions. I had been trapped behind my mask, hiding from the trauma and pain for way too long. These demons wanted to claim me as they had claimed my parents. As I sat there with this battle raging in me, I put my hand out and cried out to God. He met me in that moment. I needed my truth to find me. I needed to see the truth of who I really was.

Thankfully the voice of courage and hope came and rescued me.

That day I realized that I carried so much unforgiveness towards my dad and uncle, my aunty and mum. Right then, through many tears and sobbing, as hard as it was, I made the choice to forgive them. I knew I needed to be released from them if I was going to find myself.

If I could fully forgive them, I would be able to move past the loss, remove the labels, and put down the masks once and for all.

I made the choice to forgive, even though it was an unfair choice. I realized I had the strength, courage, and ability to make good choices.

On that day, countless emotions that had been clouding my truth and leading me into a very dark path were silenced.

I was now in control of which wave I should surf and could see the facts and the truth.

Call to Action – Emotions

As you take this journey to unmask your life, know your behavior is a direct reflection of your emotions.

Emotions will rule your responses and actions. Maybe you're like I was and reacted out of emotions without looking at the facts.

I am not saying that you need to become emotionless. I am just asking you to notice your emotions as they are occurring and take them into account before you act. Pausing to reflect does not require us all to be superhuman and in control of each and every emotion. What we need to do is identify how they affect our everyday life and decisions.

Thomas Fuller said,

> Get the facts, or the facts will get you. And when you get 'em, get 'em right, or they will get you wrong.

When we stop and look at the facts of the situation, we can see more than just emotions. We have to understand that our perspective is shaped by the filter of emotions. To keep things in perspective, we have to learn to stop, breathe, and gather as much information as we can.

On this journey, as you become more aware of your behaviors and your emotional responses and how they play out in your life, it will become clearer how they impact and dictate your life.

Emotions, when good, can be used to add value to our lives. They can give us the passion needed to create our vision for a better life, enhance our beliefs, and inspire us into action. I don't want you to overlook the good emotions in our life.

Let's use our A, B, and C system to unpack what you are feeling right now.

A	B	C
Action	**Belief**	**Choice**
Nothing will change unless you act	Belief is an inside job	Every step is a choice

Journal Prompt One

A
Action

Let's identify the circumstances that seem to be crashing over you as you try to ride them.

1. Start by writing out each time you feel those crashing waves.
2. Can you identify what triggers those crashing waves?
3. How do those emotions play out in your words, actions and daily life?

Remember, this journey of healing is a marathon, not a sprint. Continue to identify those emotional waves and triggers as needed. Today is just the starting point.

Journal Prompt Two

B
Belief

As you examine your life and your interactions with others, think about:

1. How do others respond to your emotional outbursts?
2. Do you find yourself jumping onto that emotional wave without stopping and considering the consequences?
3. Do you try to cover up those emotions? Do you make excuses for those emotional outbursts to those around you?

Don't try to process all of this at once. Start with one emotional response that is not serving you well. Look at ways you could ride this wave instead of being overtaken.

Journal Prompt Three

C
Choice

Try to identify the obstacles that are preventing you from healing. What is keeping you from moving forward? You have identified in **A** the emotional waves, the triggers, and how those traumas are playing out in your life. In **B,** you identified your responses and reactions.

Now it's time to make a choice of how you will ride your emotions and keep moving forward. Some key strategies to consider that will enable you to handle the emotions that are tripping you up are:

1. Make the decision about which emotions you are going to ride and which you will let pass by.

2. Prepare a strategy for how to look at the facts and not be sucked into the lies of negative emotions.

3. When you feel that emotional wave coming, ask yourself what is the best response to benefit from this situation.

    a. Maybe it's stepping away for a few minutes and taking time to breathe slowly.

    b. Look at the facts.

    c. Ask yourself what the truth in this situation is?

d. Remember that we judge ourselves on our intentions and others on their actions.

e. Make your decision based on being objective.

On this journey, you will build emotional discernment, and you will become proactive in handling your emotions. Remember M. Asch's statement, "Motions are the precursors of emotions." Emotions will come, but we can always choose to do something and avoid being crushed by them.

> **This is a new season, a new chapter of your life, and new chapters require new insight and understanding as they bring opportunities to overcome challenges.**

In order to move on, you must understand why you felt what you did and why you no longer need to feel it.

- MITCH ALBOM,

THE FIVE PEOPLE YOU MEET IN HEAVEN

Chapter Three

Re-mark – Movies

Let this hope of a better future give you the strength and courage you need to work through the pain and hurt, not just to survive your past, but to live victoriously in the present.

- CHRISTINE CAINE

I love movies. I especially love being able to lose myself in a dramatic scene. My favorite movies are those that echo true life moments, stories of hope, and stories of overcoming. I have to make a confession: I am also a bit of an ABBA fan and just love their movies because they combine true-life moments and great music. ABBA movies bring me joy.

I often find myself thinking about one of those great movies I watched, particularly the key words or moments that held my attention. And if I don't like the ending, I find myself rewriting it in my mind. I will plot out different endings, wondering what it would look like if it ended this way or that. I guess the writer in me always wants to be creating better stories.

Before I realized that I could unmask and live my life, I would dream about a different ending to my story. During those "what if" moments, I would play out in my mind different endings to that day when I was thirteen and many days and years after that. Each scene would start with a "What if . . .". What if I didn't hand Dad his gun? What if Dad didn't take his life? What if this didn't happen? What if my uncle had not raped me that night? What if my mum would have chosen life? What if she had been there as I grew into an adult to advise me and love me? Maybe, just maybe, my life could have a happy ending with a happy family. Countless times I would lose myself in the hope of "what if" and try to rewrite the movie of my life to create a perfect ending to my story.

Inevitably when I was lost in my daydreams of "what if," reality would hit. The movie screen in my mind would fill with death and devastation and the echo of how all those moments of distractions had impacted my life. I remained trapped in the replays of the truth of my life story.

Proverbs 23:7 (KJV) states,

> For as a man thinketh in his heart, so is he.

The thoughts of our hearts shape who we are. Our thoughts shape our thinking, which shapes our words and, ultimately, our actions. As our own movies and words replay in our minds, we lose the truth of the events.

Untruths and lies are the Bogus Stories (BS) that clutter our thoughts. BS in equals BS out. Where your thoughts go, your focus follows. Protecting our thoughts should be our highest priority, especially since our health and welfare are the by-products of those thoughts.

Neuro-Linguistic Programming acknowledges the fundamental connection between the brain (neuro) and the language (linguistic) of our words. What it shows is that our internal and external behaviors or actions (programming) are connected at a very deep level. The Neuro-Linguistic Programming school of thought considers the practical application of thought awareness as it relates to positive, healthy living.

Ironically, we always find what we are looking for. So, we must be aware of what we really are looking for in our lives. The longer we allow those replays to become what we look at, the more we will find trauma, wounds, pain, and painful circumstances in our lives.

I heard a story that best explains this idea of perspective. A hummingbird and a vulture were flying over the deserts. All the vulture saw was rotting meat because that is what he was looking for. However, the hummingbird ignored the smelly flesh of dead animals. Instead, she looked for the colorful blossoms of desert plants. The story points out that what you seek, you will find. A second lesson is that vultures live on what was. Vultures feed on the past. They fill themselves with what is dead and gone. But hummingbirds live on what is vibrant and alive. They seek new life. They feed on freshness and life. Each bird finds what it is looking for. We all do.

We all know someone who is a vulture and someone who is a hummingbird. Or maybe we have been one, if not both ourselves. Who are the vultures in your life—the people you dread running into because they speak of nothing ever being right? The vultures in our life seem to thrive on the negative. They feed on what was, hungering for rot and decay. They live in the past. Now consider the hummingbirds in your life. They are the people we look forward to seeing and being in their presence; they bring life and energy into our world.

I was a vulture in people's lives for way too long. I was living on what was, feeding on the wounds and pain of the past. The past was all I used as the filter for my life and my value. In every situation, I want to find the rot, the decay, and the ugly because, for so long, it had been all I knew to feed on. In the happiest, brightest moments of my life, I would find or create darkness. That's what vulture people do.

The story of the vulture and the hummingbird reminds me to be very careful about what I should look for in life.

> Your eye is like a lamp that provides light for your body. When your eye is healthy, your whole body is filled with light.
>
> **(MATTHEW 6:22 NLT)**

What are the movies you're replaying in your life? Are there parts of your story you want to rewrite? Are there parts that you keep replaying in a continuous loop, focusing only on the "what if?" Are those old, worn-out movies and thoughts keeping you trapped and distracting you from moving forward?

The truth is that when we replay these movies of pain, destruction, and despair, hoping for a different ending allows our energy to become fixed on the negative. Focusing on the "what ifs" does not change anything. When despair overtakes hope, it blinds us to any promise of the future we were born to have. As hard as it can be, we must be able to accept what's done is done, that we can't change the past through "what-ifs," and there are no do-overs.

CS Lewis said,

> You can't go back and change the beginning, but you can start where you are and change the ending.

We can become so attached to the emotion of our past that we miss the facts. Over time you start to believe the emotions of shame and guilt as your truth. Each replay moves you back into the emotions of the trauma and the pain of the past. These replays are not an account of an actual event. Instead, they are your recollection of the event, often layered with your emotions and other people's story of the event. My story of the rape was twisted by my aunt's story that what happened was my fault and I should be ashamed instead of scared. The story that has you trapped in a powerless loop has probably been shaped by what others said or how they reacted. Remember, what we empower will devour us. It's vital to understand that these replays aren't a reflection of reality; they are simply the result of a survival process to make sense of what happened.

> **The story we call our truth is built with broken pieces, misplaced emotions, and broken people, and not the truth. Accepting this will allow you to turn your tears into courage.**

In the legal system, when a judge is summing up for a jury the evidence of a trial, the judge reminds them not to get caught up in the emotion of the case but to look at the facts and, from there, find the truth. No matter what your life story is, no matter the movies you keep playing over and over, hoping for a different ending, if you want to move forward and unmask your life, it's time to stop hitting replay on that movie! It is time to create a new story line for the next chapter of your life.

In a trial, the jury can be faced with deciding between life and death, or freedom or jail for life. Guess what? The decision you make about what is true can mean the difference between life and death for you as well.

I love this quote from Jim Rohan,

> If you change, everything will change for you.

In other words, if I want my life to change, then it needs to start with me. Up until my turning point, I had been empowering the hurt, shame, guilt, and worthlessness that came from the suicide, violence, and rape in my home. I was letting my past dictate who I could become, how I viewed life, and what I believed about myself. As far as I could see, my life would end the same way as my parents' lives: empty, alone, and in despair. It was time for me to let what God did for me be bigger than what's been done to me.

I recently read, "If you erase all the mistakes of your past, you will erase all the wisdom of your present. Remember the lesson, not the disappointment."

So often, when I speak, I'm asked, "If you could, what would you change in your life?" Without hesitation, I always say, "I would not change a thing. As hard as it has been, it makes me who I am today." I would not wish my story on anyone else, but I equally would not change it. If I had not made the decision to take the action I needed to take to bring about the change I wanted, I am sure my answer would be different.

We all have a story, and when we tell that story from a point of healing, not as a victim, it will empower us and others to use that story to help others conquer their past and live victoriously in the present. A healed story is a much better movie to replay over in your mind!

> Let the inner movement of your heart always be to love one another, and never play the role of an actor wearing a mask.
>
> **(ROMANS 12:9 TPT)**

I have had the privilege and joy of visiting Ukraine and working with some of the precious women there. On one visit, I remember driving two hours in a car that was missing parts of the floor. That's right. I could see the road racing past me, between my feet, as we drove to a little building filled with people from a little Ukrainian mining town. That town has since been demolished in the war between Ukraine and Russia, which absolutely breaks my heart. What happened to all the women I taught?

In that now-lost Ukrainian mining town, I shared my story of trauma from the perspective of the healing journey I was on. At the end of my story, a lady in the audience came to me and told me she had planned to go home that day to take her life as she had been living with the feeling of hopelessness for too long. This lady went on to tell me that someone had invited her to come to this meeting. With tears in her eyes, she told me that my story of how I found my way through gave her hope not to give up but keep going.

You will never know who is needing to hear your story—be sure to tell it from a point of victory.

No matter where you are on this journey, today can be the start of building a life story that one day you will be able to share from a point of healing and victory. Your new story starts with the next step you take, the next choice you make. Just simply start where you are. Start living your life in a way that is worth telling stories about.

Precious ones, it's time to write a new chapter, create that new movie, a new narrative of who you want to be. You are uniquely created with a purpose. There has never been and never will be anyone like you. You matter. What you do matters. Your story matters!

When it comes to making a positive difference in your life, that change will only occur when you take responsibility for the change and take the action required for that difference to become your new reality.

Call to Action – Movies

I know crossing over the bridge and leaving the familiar can cause fear to rise. This is where you need to dig deep and find the courage to look fear in the eye and say, "I see you, but I am moving forward anyway."

Putting a stop to that old negative movie that is trapping you in that dark place is a big step. Marathons have mountains to climb, and this is one of them. If you want this new, better chapter to be unlike the past, the story line needs to change. This next step is needed. Yes, it will be scary, but anything less is maintaining the status quo.

As you unpack those thoughts and old stories that keep you trapped, let me continue to encourage you to use a journal to document your journey and help you with the healing process.

Use your:

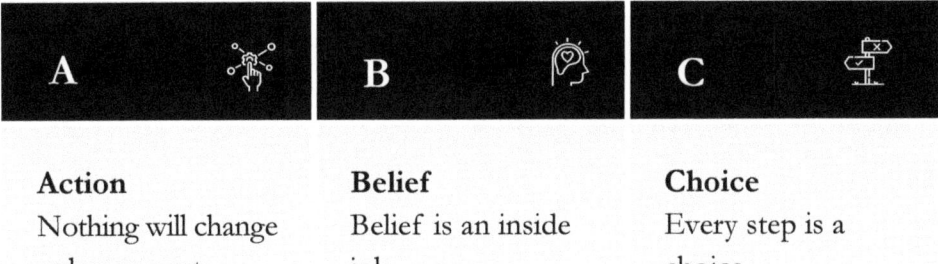

A	**B**	**C**
Action	**Belief**	**Choice**
Nothing will change unless you act	Belief is an inside job	Every step is a choice

Journal Prompt One

A___

Action

Take the time starting today to identify the behavior patterns that keep taking you back to those old, dark wounds. These patterns can become habits that keep us from our true purpose and destiny.

1. Can you identify what the trigger is that keeps taking you back?
2. Can you identify if it's guilt or shame that is keeping you there? It is important to know the difference.

> *Sow a thought, reap an action.*
> *Sow an action, reap a habit.*
> *Sow a habit, reap character.*
> *Sow character, reap a destiny.*

Take your time. Remember, this is a marathon, not a sprint.

Journal Prompt Two

B

Belief

Please allow yourself the time to think intently during this next section as we look deeper into shame and guilt.

Brené Brown's definitions of shame and guilt will help you understand the difference. She says, "Guilt says, 'You've done something wrong,' or 'You've made a bad choice,' where shame says, 'You are a bad person.'"

If you feel guilt for a decision you made, accept that you can't do it over. It's imperative to remember that just because you have made a mistake does not mean that you are a mistake.

Your ability to admit you made a mistake does make you vulnerable. But as the best-selling author Brené Brown has taught us, to be vulnerable is to have courage.

Carrying shame indicates that what you are focused on is a deep wound that needs to be healed. Shame feeds on the belief that we are not okay with who we are. Shame is a powerful emotion that you need to address so that wound is healed.

1. If you're experiencing guilt, it is time to forgive yourself. Admit your true role and responsibility, and let it go.
2. If you're experiencing shame, separate the emotions from the facts. Find your truth and hold on to that.

Use your "I choose to know" statements:

- I choose to know that I am not a mistake.
- I choose to walk free of guilt and shame; they are not who I am.
- I choose to know that I am worthy.

Journal Prompt Three

C
Choice

Brené Brown says it well: "People who wade through discomfort and vulnerability and tell the truth about their stories are the real badasses in this world." Please be totally honest with yourself. Use your journal to tell yourself the truth, your truth.

1. As you are journaling, think of the facts and not the emotions of those past traumas. What are the facts, minus the emotions, telling you?
2. What action do you need to take so you can hit stop on the old movies that are keeping you trapped?
   a. Identify what drags you back into those old negative movies and keeps you trapped in that place. Identifying these triggers enables you to avoid or neutralize them.
   b. Where do you need to dig up the courage and make the choice to say, "Enough is enough, what's done is done!"?
   c. How can you create a new habit? When those negative thoughts come to your mind, have an "I choose to know" statement ready to tell yourself the truth.

I choose to know that just because I made a bad choice does not make me bad!

I choose to know that I can move forward because I was created for more than this!

Your identity emerges out of your daily habits, and every choice you make is a step on the path toward who you want to become.

> The truth is, unless you let go, unless you forgive yourself, unless you forgive the situation, unless you realize that the situation is over, you cannot move forward.
>
> **– STEVE MARABOLI**

Hummingbirds live on what is vibrant and alive.
They seek new life.
They feed on freshness and life.
Each bird finds what it is looking for.
Today is the day!
You can do this!

Chapter Four

Re-mark – Attitude

> Our attitude cannot stop our emotions or feelings, but it can stop our emotions and feelings from stopping us.

I love the value of attitude. On my journey of healing, my attitude was one of the first things I needed to change. What I love about attitude is that when I made a decision to work on this simple thing (maybe not so easy but simple), I saw instant results.

As you become the central character of your new story, the essential component of that new character is managing your attitude, which will be a game changer for you. As you grow your understanding of the power of attitude and the difference that your attitude can make in your journey, taking the time to reflect on how your attitude impacts your behaviors and actions will be key.

What if you are just one decision away from a totally different life?

What if that decision is a decision to work on your attitude?

Your attitude will play a major role in unmasking your life and will be the difference maker in your re-marked life more than anything else. As you completed your A, B, and C prompts in the previous chapter, you decided to hit "stop" on those negative movie replays. When fear rears its ugly head, adopt an attitude of "no more." No more will fear control you now that you have the power to look fear in the face and say, "I see you. I am not going to back down or step away."

The attitude you choose can have you feeding your fear. Our attitude colors what we see and how we see it. Attitude starts in your heart, filters through your beliefs, and then comes out of your mouth. My old attitude was so bitter and resentful about the life I lived, the wounds, the shame, and the guilt. I was always blaming everyone for what had happened to me. My attitude had gotten to the point that all that those close to me saw, felt, and experienced was an angry, bitter, unhappy woman.

I lived my victim status fully and loudly. I let it guide my words and actions. My victim beliefs tainted my attitude and oozed from my wounds. I was not pleasant to be around with my mask off. Out in the "real" world with my mask securely in place, I was as pleasant and polite as could be. No one knew about the angry, broken, bitter woman living behind the mask. They just saw a well-dressed, well made-up, got-it-all-together mask-wearing me.

Your traumas, wounds, missteps, and circumstances do not dictate the future. Other people's experiences, fears, beliefs, and words don't determine your future. You get to decide what you do. You have the choice to let your mind run on autopilot, aligning with fear, or flip the switch on your attitude and start becoming who you want to be.

Being accountable for the attitude and actions you take is a decision you make daily. Attitude is tied to our emotions and our beliefs and creates our circumstances. When we experience an inability to escape the trauma, we often perceive ourselves as a failure and develop an attitude of failure rather than separate ourselves from those experiences. We become one with that fear and attach ourselves to that failure. Fear is a hungry beast that feeds on itself and grows. The stronger that fear grows, the more it plays out in our attitude.

Fear and the sense of failure can cripple us. In January 2017, on a trip to Fiji with my husband, daughter, son-in-law, and two grandchildren, my daughter announced, "Mum, we are all going to go zip lining." Zip lining is when you allow a stranger who took a 10-minute training, strap you into a harness hooked to cables strung 100 feet over an open, rocky cliff and then tell you to relax as they push you out into a great gap where suddenly you hang above the forest while everyone else is still safely on the platform shouting, "Have fun!" OH, and you pay for this experience.

So, when my daughter announced that, as a family, we were going to have a zip-line adventure, fear rose up in me. Here I was, working hard on my journey of growth, trust, and faith and learning how to look fear in the face as my daughter, without realizing it, tossed this zip-line adventure and challenged me. My attitude of failure kicked in. I was thinking to myself; *I can't do this. It's impossible for me. I am way too old for this. This is crazy.* Without realizing it, I was setting myself up for failure by empowering my fear.

When I took a moment and reflected on what it was that I feared about the zip-line adventure, I realized that I didn't want to look foolish. The idea of hanging in a harness, feet dangling hundreds of feet above the treetops, made me feel insecure. Instead of sharing the nature of my fear with my daughter, I picked up my mask of "having it all together" and said, "Sure, I can do that"—all the time, knowing and believing that I couldn't. On the drive to the zip-line station, my negative self-talk was going strong, and with each mile that passed, I found more and more ways to empower my fear.

My self-talk was creating a self-fulfilling prophecy—a prophecy that I would be a failure.

Fear hides behind many different faces. Fear also loves to use its little demon voices to stop us in our tracks. Those little dark voices in our heads whisper things like, "You can't do this" or "You're not good enough." Public failure was not an option for me. I had worked so hard at being in control and perfect. Zip-lining offered no way to appear perfect or in control.

My athletic daughter, not being one to back down from a challenge, loaded us all into the bus that was going to take us to the top of the hill. As we drove out into the bush, where the zip lines are strung through trees over deep chasms, my mind raced. When my husband said, "Count me out," my six-year-old granddaughter decided to stay with him. My fear became so tangible that I could taste it in my mouth, and there seemed to be no way to bow out gracefully.

We all got harnessed up and put our helmets on, and I took my glasses off, thinking I needed to keep them safe for a couple of reasons: 1. I did not want to drop them as I swung between the trees, and 2. deep down, I did not want to know where I was going. We headed up the side of a hill to a long platform to get hooked onto the zip line.

Fear was flowing in every part of me. My heart was racing. I knew in every fiber of my body that I would fail, and everyone would have a good laugh at my failure. Have you ever felt like that? My attitude and negative emotions were oozing everywhere, echoing out into the group. Everyone was standing on the platform, laughing and teasing each other as they waited to be hooked up.

Standing on the platform hundreds of feet in the air, I saw my ten-year-old grandson laughing and hanging upside down, zipping high above the trees, and I then realized it was my turn next!

Fear deafened me to the last-minute instructions I was being given. Then suddenly, I was pushed off the platform. Surprise, surprise, I failed. How do you fail at zip lining? I guess I didn't jump high enough and had not gotten enough momentum because I was too scared to move. And my fear of momentum worked against me. You see, I got three feet from the platform and came to a stop. I could not go forward, nor could I go back on my own. Instead, I had to be pulled back to the platform and try again.

One thing you need to know with this zip-line course is that once you commit to going, there is no coming back; the only way down and back to safety is to reach each of the five platforms scattered through the canyon. And each platform takes you higher and stretches out longer.

It seemed that each section got worse. My attitude of fear and self-doubt was spilling everywhere, and by the time I got unhooked from the harness, I was done! I was crying, and I felt like a total failure. What I had feared had come true. When I arrived back to where my husband and granddaughter were sitting, I had moved past fear to full-out anger. I was angry at myself for even trying, angry for doing something I knew I would fail at, and even angry at my daughter for challenging me. No one was safe from my anger and my attitude at that moment.

Out of the corner of my eye, I saw my daughter walking up to me. As she approached, it was clear that she could see my tear-stained face. Putting her arms around me, she whispered, "It's okay, Mum, you did well. You had a good go at it. You're safe." She spoke those words hoping to console me. Instead of consoling me, she triggered my lack of self-belief. "You had a go, but you failed. You're not up to this," is what I heard.

How many times have you said to someone else or to yourself, "That's okay, you had a go" as an excuse for not trying again, or "That's okay, I knew I would fail?" Failure is not final unless you choose not to get back up. On this journey, it's your staying power that counts, not how many times you slip, fall, stumble, or go off track. We can get so caught up in the emotions of failure that we forget to look at the facts.

Hearing the excitement of watching her brother on the lines and seeing his fun, my little granddaughter insisted that she was "in." My granddaughter was so quick to overcome her fear. She demanded we all climb back up the mountain, harness back up, and "do it again." Feeling totally beaten and defeated, I decided to stay with my husband, where I could keep my feet on the ground. Fear and my bad attitude had won. I was defeated and a failure, again.

My private decisions become public outcomes. I had to decide to continue to stay in that place of feeling like a failure. My poor attitude fed my belief that new things are bad things and new opportunities never work out. My fear and my rotten attitude and emotions had decreed my decisions way too much. Now it was time to conquer this next one. Could I find the courage to overcome this zip line thing and step up and go again with a different attitude?

All of this, along with the following questions, were racing through my mind:

- What sort of example was I for my grandchildren?
- If I did not face this fear and push through this BS, what would happen the next time?
- If I went again, was I doing it for me or to be able to wear the mask of courage and impress my daughter?
- Could I believe in myself enough to change my attitude and own my responsibility to myself?

> **Experience is not the best teacher; evaluated experience is. You get to decide if that experience is good or bad. Fear of the future or the unknown is a natural response. Confidence comes from having a go and evaluating that experience.**

Champions fall and yes, even fail; they also stumble and ask for help where needed, but they get back up and have another go. That's what makes them champions. After this experience, I could look back and say either, "Well, I tried, I knew I would fail, and I did" or "I learned what I needed to know from that experience, and I will give it another go, in a different way."

I love this quote from my mentor John C. Maxwell:

> Your attitude towards failure determines your altitude after failure.

Did I want to believe that I was a failure? Did I want to accept the lie that it was impossible for me to succeed? My life changed while I stood watching my granddaughter head up the trail. You may be laughing and saying, "Come on, Wendy, it's only a zip line. This zip line experience became my watermark for how I would face fear and self-doubt.

I pulled all the courage I could find, called out to my granddaughter, and shouted, "Wait for me!" You see, I decided to harness up again and head off up to the zip line. This time there was a difference—my attitude was different. I told myself that it was possible and that I would prove not to my daughter but to myself that I could succeed. I looked fear in the eye and said, "I see you, but I am doing this anyway." And this time I put my glasses on because when we jumped off the platform and into the wide-open space, I wanted to see everything in my future.

This leap from the platform—a slightly awkward leap, I might add—was what I needed to do for me, no one else. I needed to overcome my old story of fear and failure. I needed to break free of my old self. I had a choice, and I took it. I chose courage and to push through the BS.

By the way, this time, I was right on my granddaughter's heels off the platform.

It's not whether you go down but how you come back up that counts. Our attitude will always be the difference maker.

That day was one of those steep, uphill climbs on this marathon race of life, a day that only I could be responsible for. You and I each have the ability to choose our response and the ability to make a choice.

Your attitude is a choice you make.

Your attitude affects your outlook.

Your attitude always precedes your actions.

Your attitude alters your outcomes.

Your attitude will feed fear or feed courage.

Remember, your attitude is one thing you can always control, and it will be the difference-maker in your story!

> Success is not final; failure is not fatal; it is the courage to continue that counts.
>
> - **WINSTON S. CHURCHILL.**

Call to Action – Attitude

Our attitude is not fixed. We can change our attitude at will. In my zip line story, I set my attitude for failure the minute my daughter announced we were going zip-lining. My poor, debilitating attitude dictated my decisions and fed my fears, and it showed up in me getting stuck. A change of attitude changes the outcome, as my granddaughter demonstrated that day.

As you examine the attitudes that color and impact your everyday life, let me encourage you to continue to use your journal to document your journey and help you with the healing process.

Use your:

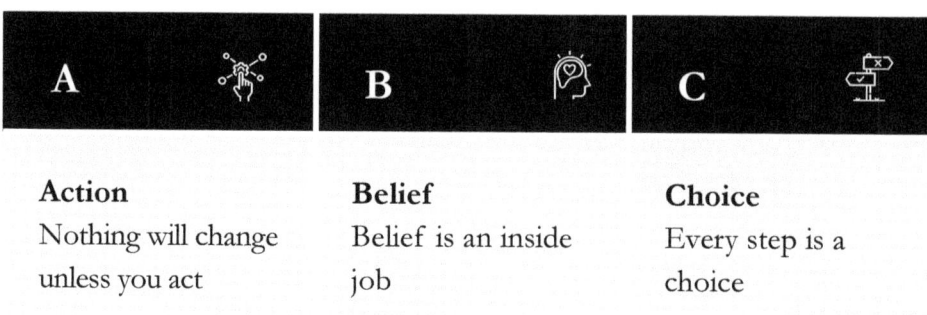

Action	**Belief**	**Choice**
Nothing will change unless you act	Belief is an inside job	Every step is a choice

Journal Prompt One

A

Action

Take your time as you work through these questions.

1. Can you see a poor attitude that is currently coloring everything around you?
2. Journal on how your attitudes affect and infect you and those around you and your actions.
3. Do attitudes feed your fear?
4. Can you see where your attitudes hold you back and limit your potential, your dreams, your hopes, and your future? Write down your observations.

Journal Prompt Two

B

Belief

In A, you looked at your attitude and its effects on your life. It's just as important to re-mark your life for your new story. This is the time for a new understanding of how your attitude and thinking will impact your story going forward.

1. Imagine, for a moment, having a different attitude, an attitude of empowerment in yourself. What would that attitude look like?

2. How will you face fear differently moving forward?

3. What will it feel like to step out into the dreams of your future with an attitude of "anything is possible?"

Journal Prompt Three

C
Choice

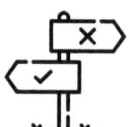

Decide on a simple, one-step action to move forward—one step to step up to your zip line with.

1. As you work to turn your attitude around, what is one thing you can do beginning today to master a new attitude?

2. What would your future be like, and how would others experience you if your attitude toward certain things were different?

It's good to start with one step at a time, then move to the next thing.

> **Small steps over time lead to great change.**

We can affect our future by being aware and taking control of our attitude, which forms our beliefs and controls our thinking. What we think about today and our attitude, is what we become tomorrow.

I want my children, grandchildren, and generations to come to know what I lived for. I want them to know that I turned my "what if" fears into "what if" opportunities to empower them on this journey of life.

I mentioned that fear has many different faces to hide its identity, and fear loves to use its little voices to stop us in our tracks. Those little voices in our head whisper things like, "You can't do this" or "You're not good enough."

The truth is, it's okay to stumble and fall on your journey. The scrapes and bruises will take us closer to victory.

In life, all of us will hesitate, misstep, and fail, but failing does not make us a failure. *What if* you flip the script on fear? *What if* you look at fear as such a great opportunity to grow? *What if* you were more fearful of missed opportunities than potential failures? *What if* you saw those fearful moments through eyes of gratitude for the opportunity to grow? *What if!*

> When the negative thoughts come—and they will; they come to all of us—it's not enough to just not dwell on it, you've got to replace it with a positive thought.
>
> **- JOEL OSTEEN.**

I am cheering you on, dear one…

Chapter Five

Re-mark – Regret

We never know what or who hangs in the balance of the decisions we make. But we do know that our decisions determine the direction and quality of our life.

- ANDY STANLEY.

The *Cambridge Dictionary* defines "regret" as "a feeling of sadness about something sad or wrong or about a mistake that you have made, and a wish that it could have been different and better."

The Prison of Regret is that place you visit over and over for the same mistake. However it's not a place to visit and certainly not a place to live permanently. Being regretful is fine; living in regret is a choice of fear and shame.

Regret becomes destructive when you are absorbed by it. When you live in regret, you become fixated on how an event from the past could be changed in a way to produce a more desirable outcome. Regret often involves imagining the ways your life might have gone differently.

Regret can have incredibly painful emotions attached to it. While regret is rooted in feelings of remorse, disappointment, guilt, or sorrow for things that have happened in the past, such feelings can have a powerful influence over your life. Regret eats away the human heart just as surely as any other disease eats away at human flesh. Living in the belief that we could have changed the past if only we had known better will create frustration and sorrow and become our daily food.

Regret thrives where there is no power to forgive yourself, to receive forgiveness, and/or to forgive another person. The problem is that when you are feeling regret over past mistakes, you miss out on the joys of the present moment. The Prison of Regret, like the movies in our mind, keeps us living in agreement with the pain, guilt, shame, and sorrow over what that regret is about.

Regret can also trigger wounds that have lain dormant. Before we know it, we find those wounds rearing their ugly head. It's so important to remember that no one is immune to feelings of regret.

The trap of regret is something each of us must be mindful of. On your journey of life, without awareness, it's so easy to take the wrong track and land smack bang in the Prison of Regret without even realizing it. When we do find ourselves locked in regret, we must work hard to escape. Regret can be all-consuming and it will destroy your life if you're not managing to move past it.

We can be living with regret over something we have no control over fixing, or we can take control of those things we can change and take up the courage to face a new situation.

I carried regret about my dad, uncle, aunt, and mum for way too long in my life. Those old unchangeable movies played over and over in my mind, and the more I watched them, the more I felt I could have changed the outcome if only I had ... The more I believed I had control over the past, the more regret I lived with.

My dad, uncle, aunt, and mum are all dead. They will never acknowledge how their selfish acts wounded me. There will be no chance for them to say sorry for what they did to me or how their actions impacted my life. They will hold no sorrow for the trauma, pain, and wounds they caused. I will never hear them asking for forgiveness. If I'd stayed in that place of regret, nothing was going to change. For me to have the life that I was worthy of, I needed to reach a level of reconciliation with those events on my own. I had to reach a place of being ok with the fact that what was done was done.

There was no going back if I was to escape this prison.

If I was to receive healing, then I needed to heal myself. How did I begin to move past the regret? I used the power of writing, and I asked Jesus to help me forgive those that had harmed me so deeply. The torment I was living in had to stop. I was the only person who could take the action to make it stop. I used words like "I choose not to blame or hold the actions of (name) against him/her," and "Where I have felt betrayed by them, I forgive them." Also, to fully release myself, I had to forgive myself.

None of us are immune to regret. About two years ago, my husband and I made a life-changing decision to pack up and move from Queensland to the Northern Territory. This was not a little move down the road a few miles. No, it required we move completely across the county. We downsized everything we owned to make this big move. We felt strongly in our hearts it was the right move for us.

We were also aware that our decision would impact the family we were leaving. We were leaving one set of family members to be closer to other family members. This is not about the right or wrong of the decision but about how quickly I entered the Prison of Regret after all the healing I thought I had done that made me think I was immune.

Andy Stanley explains it like this, "We never know what or who hangs in the balance of the decisions. But what we do know is that private decisions have public outcomes. Your private decisions probably won't stay private. Your personal decisions will impact some other persons."

Our Queensland family's sadness was a result of our decision, and emotions were running high. When emotions run high, we can get caught up in the emotions, and our focus turns inward. I felt misunderstood, and I allowed that feeling of being misunderstood to flow out in my words and behavior. You would think I would know better. After all, I teach this stuff. But none of us, no one, is immune. We are always on a continual learning loop if we choose to learn from life lessons.

It took a few months for our big move to happen, and it was not an easy time for anyone. The move itself was gigantic, but little did I know that I had packed a big dose of regret into those boxes. As I opened each box, I was drawn deeper into the Prison of Regret. It did not matter that I knew being in Darwin was where we were meant to be.

For the first nine months of our new life in Darwin, I wasn't sleeping and I was constantly in tears, replaying the movie of "if only I did this or didn't do that." I walked through those nine months wearing a mask of "I'm ok, everything is fine," when in fact, I was in pain, overflowing with regret. This pain and regret were impacting my physical and emotional health. This regret was not about the move—we were in the right place—but about my role in how my choices impacted my relationships and the family we'd left behind.

How was I able to move past this regret? I found one person with whom I could share my feelings and talk about my overwhelming regret. That person turned out to be my eldest daughter. While I sat there on the phone with her sobbing, in a space free of any judgment, she became the person that kept reminding me that I had the power to leave the Prison of Regret. She pushed me to remember that I always knew what to do. What I'd coached my clients to do was now what I was required to do. This time I needed someone to remind me that I was courageous enough to find my way out.

There comes a time when each of us must decide enough is enough, that we will no longer allow regret to be part of our lives. I needed to start taking the steps to find my way out of this deep wound caused by the regret over moving.

A lot of regrets that we choose to live with are unnecessary.

My moving forward and out of regret started with a courageous conversation. I decided to ask for forgiveness from those that were harmed by our move. I owned my actions and behaviors but not theirs. Often if you take that first step, you will find, as I did, that the other person has already moved on, and in their mind, everything is okay. When we are stuck in that Prison of Regret, our fears and self-doubt replay in a loop in our heads, and that loop can blow a situation all out of proportion. When we escape the Prison of Regret, it's like pushing a stop button on that loop of regret.

I want to add a caution: If someone is still living that has hurt you, or you know you have hurt, but you are aware that there is a risk to your safety, you don't have to physically put yourself in an unsafe space. Your first responsibility is to yourself and to remain safe. You will know who is safe and who is not, and if you're unsure, err on the side of unsafe. In those unsafe situations, use your journal. For example, I wrote letters of forgiveness to my dad, mum, uncle, and aunty and also to myself. After writing these letters, then I spoke out loud the words of forgiveness. Also, praying for release is a powerful tool in working through forgiveness.

There is a lot of unnecessary regret in our lives that we can rectify to begin living with peace about a situation. Remember

> **What we empower will devour us.**

To avoid being in a place of regret, start by recognizing when you have gone off track and crashed into the Prison of Regret. Once you recognize you're sliding off track, take the steps you need to find your way out by following the journaling ABCs.

Regret will echo in our lives until it is addressed head-on. Living with regret limits our ability to fully live in our purpose.

To unmask and live your life of purpose is about taking one step, then the next, slowly and intentionally. As you take those steps, keep your eyes on the future, and walk with your destiny in mind until you leave the dreaded Prison of Regret.

> **Regret is a living power that torments us and reminds us of pain. It takes courage to face it every time.**

Call to Action – Regret

Regret is a big step to work through. Let me encourage you to continue to document your journey in your journal to support your healing.

As you go through this process, if you need to talk with someone, I encourage you to identify someone you can trust that will listen to you and support you without judgment. No one can take these steps for you, but they can walk alongside you. Action creates ownership, and it's your action that will bring you out of the Prison of Regret.

Use your:

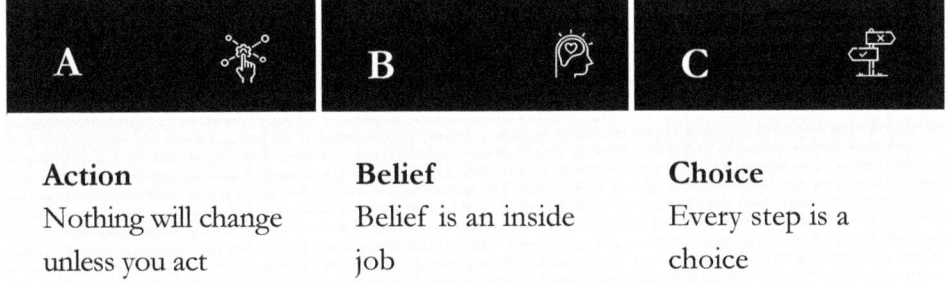

A	**B**	**C**
Action	**Belief**	**Choice**
Nothing will change unless you act	Belief is an inside job	Every step is a choice

Journal Prompt One

A

Action

Let me remind you that regret is a living power that feeds off the places in our lives where we are seeking validation, acceptance, forgiveness, and even love.

Start with healing one regret at a time. Please don't try to work on them all at once.

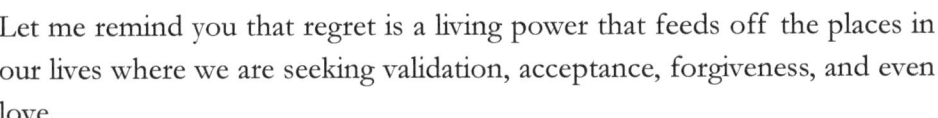

1. Identify one thing that keeps you in that Prison of Regret.
2. How did you get here?
3. What is the truth of the situation?
4. Is it safe to seek forgiveness and resolution face-to-face?
5. What would a resolution look like for you?
6. What one step could you take to move towards resolution?

Be as specific as possible.

Take your time with this.

Pick one regret that you can talk about safely with that person face-to-face to achieve forgiveness. Then work through how that conversation will go in your journal. Remember my caution above as you make this decision.

If you'll be meeting with that person face-to-face, use your journal to work through the conversation first to help you separate the facts from the emotions. If this regret is one that you need to work through on your own, let me encourage you to use the forgiveness steps to support you in walking free from this regret.

Remember, the aim is to solve the regret and to live unmasked.

Your statement of forgiveness could look like this:

"I choose not to blame or hold the actions of (name) against him/her. Where I have felt betrayed by (name), I forgive them."

"I choose to forgive myself for any role I played for holding onto the wound."

"I choose to no longer blame myself for any role I played in (circumstance) with (name). Where I have carried shame/guilt/name, I forgive myself."

Journal Prompt Two

B
___

Belief

Start by believing that you have the capacity to live free of regret.

Answer these questions in your journal:

1. What will you gain by continuing to live with this regret?
2. What will be different by not living with this regret?
3. What are you missing out on by staying in the Prison of Regret?
4. What will be one benefit of breaking free from the Prison of Regret?

Take your time to answer these questions.

Journal Prompt Three

C
___

Choice

Once you have finished with A and B, it's time to move to C. Regret is about moving backward into old memories and old wounds. Digging deep to stand against that habit of choosing regret over forgiveness is making a choice of courage as you re-mark your life.

Just like you looked fear in the eye, now it is time to look regret in the eye and say, "I see you, regret, but I choose to move past you into forgiveness and on to freedom. I am NOT going to live with you anymore."

Making the decision that you're not going to live with regret any longer is a choice, a choice of courage.

You may have to repeat your "I choose to know" statements several times as you break free of those old regrets. For example:

1. I choose to know that I am no longer going to live with regret!
2. I choose to know forgiveness, not regret.

Repeat your "I choose to know" statement every time regret tries to occupy your mind.

Take your time working through your A, B, and C of regret.

Focus on one regret at a time and know that is enough.

If at any stage you don't feel safe, be sure to get the support you need. Talk with a trusted friend or counselor.

An unmasked you is strong and courageous because you traded regret for forgiveness.

> Keep your thoughts continually fixed on all that is authentic and real, honorable and admirable, beautiful and respectful, pure and holy, merciful and kind.
>
> **– PHILIPPIANS 4:8 TPT**

Chapter Six

Re-mark – Keep Going

Transformation is a process, and as life happens, there are tons of ups and downs. It's a journey of discovery—there are moments on mountaintops and moments in deep valleys of despair.

- RICK WARREN.

Despair brings a sense that we can't go on and are overwhelmed. It comes in many forms, from internal thoughts and feelings as well as from external factors and people. Those external factors can be words of rejection, blame or shame from others, or words and thoughts we speak over and think about ourselves, thus allowing hopelessness to creep in. This despair creates a hurdle, a hurdle that you feel you can't get over or go around and that distracts you and takes you well off track and into the wilderness.

From the minute you start this journey and for the rest of your life, remember that your growth never stops. If it did, you would become stagnant. Having a greater level of awareness of what is happening around you and in you is essential and critical. By becoming aware of any weariness creeping in, and the need to keep going and keep growing, you move closer to who you are called to be.

There were many times on my unmasking journey when I almost gave up. The climb seemed too high and too hard and moving past the hurdles seemed impossible. There were times when the energy to keep going felt like it didn't exist, where there was no joy in this journey. I knew I just needed to take the next step, but I kept hearing, "Stop. It's over; you can't go any further. You've reached your limit." Deep in my heart, I just knew that if I gave up, the rest of my life would remain unwritten, and my legacy would not be what I knew it could be. If I made excuses and allowed my negative feelings to take control, then the growth and change that could come as I unmask would lay dormant.

This chapter is written to empower you on this journey and beyond, to enable you to armor up on this journey. I am going to give you four essential items that are necessary for your journey. Our identity emerges out of our daily habits; these daily essentials, as they become habitual, will shape your unmasked life.

> Everything begins with a decision. Then, you have to manage that decision for the rest of your life.
>
> - JOHN C. MAXWELL

Essential Item One

Thinking Matters, Words Matter

How you think and what you say to yourself matters. Self-talk can take you out of this race if you allow it.

Our thoughts and the words we say to ourselves are powerful and determine our destiny, and our destiny determines our legacy. James Allen said it well, "You are today where your thoughts have brought you. You will be tomorrow where your thoughts take you." There is a battlefield in our minds. Your life will always move in the direction of your strongest thoughts. Where your thoughts go, your focus goes, and that's where you go. Hence the need to armor up with life-giving thoughts, keep going on this journey and take back control of your thinking.

Thoughts always precede action. Hope with intentional action is essential on this journey. Action creates ownership. Thoughts + Hope + Action + Ownership is a key I used and still use daily on my journey. Let me say it this way; Thoughts = Emotions = Actions = Results.

If we take control of our thoughts, we can change our future. At those times when I was worn out, beaten down, and about to give up, my thoughts focused on being defeated. My focus was on the thought, "I can't do this anymore," instead of "I can take the next step, make the next right decision."

If your thoughts are keeping you trapped in a cycle of two steps forward and six steps back, remind yourself that your thoughts matter, as out of the abundance of our thoughts flow our words. The thoughts and feelings you are focusing on will shape the reality of who you are. They shape your thinking, which will eventually shape your words and, consequently, your actions. What you say matters, but what you think matters even more.

For as [a man] thinks in his heart, so is he

(PROVERBS 23:7 NKJV).

Be aware of your thoughts and words. And to break out of that loop, change what you focus your thoughts on.

It is important to ask yourself how often you allow harmful self-talk to play around in your head and create distorted and false beliefs about who you are. This was a biggie for me. You see, I was busy telling myself that I could not go on, that I was useless, that I would not amount to anything and that I would simply end up living a life like my parents. Harmful self-talk can destroy the potential in each of us and prevent us from living fully in our destiny. Let me encourage you to become alert to those negative, crippling, momentum-stopping thoughts quickly, and take control to stop them when they pop up. Just like the movies in chapter three where you learned to hit stop on those things replaying in your mind, it is as important to hit stop on the negative thoughts and reframe them to a true declaration of power.

From my experience, that toxic self-talk always starts with the story you tell yourself about your circumstances. If you feed yourself a line about failure, or if you let trepidation rule your response, you can become so stuck that when facing an obstacle, you believe you are unable to get past it. You could probably see the number of hurdles and obstacles I built to block myself from being able to do something in that zip-line story. When you have an awareness of how you talk to yourself when you face an obstacle, you understand that it's not the obstacle that holds you back but rather what you choose to say about that obstacle.

One of my great discoveries on this journey is that there is

> **Nothing as powerful as a mind that has made up an excuse.**

Our thought life is like a train station. We can choose what train to jump on and, yes, even jump tracks to another train. We don't have to let the train control where we go mentally and emotionally.

We have the power of choice to control what we think and, subsequently, the power to control who we become. Beware of your train of thought and what destination those thoughts will take you. Remember, it's a choice. You can jump tracks and change your train of thought every time you need to. Choose thoughts that are life-giving.

Self-defeating words can infect our wounds and cause decay, oozing toxic yuck into every area of our life. My healing words of choice are God's words; for you, it may be a quote or poem that makes you feel safe and powerful.

Let me share my favorite words that keep me strong daily:

> You are so intimately aware of me, Lord. You read my heart like an open book, and you know all the words I'm about to speak before I even start a sentence! You know every step I will take before my journey even begins. You've gone into my future to prepare the way, and in kindness, you follow behind me to spare me from the harm of my past. You have laid your hand on me!
>
> **- PSALM 139:3-5 TPT**

These words empowered my journey with the hope of a better future. I pray they do yours as well.

You can also use your "I choose to know" statements to discover and declare the truth about yourself. Whatever words you choose to use, let them become a strong wall of protection around your heart. Making the effort to guard your heart and your thoughts will help you to respect yourself and cause others to respect you. Fortified walls, or as some call them, personal boundaries, will keep you strong on this journey and enable you to keep going. Take time each day to reflect and re-evaluate how you are thinking and how your words are impacting your journey. You can use your journal for this.

Remember your "I choose to know statements" stating the truth of who you are and use them daily.

> **"I choose to know that I am strong and courageous."**

My "I choose to know" statements are always close at hand. I use them in the morning, throughout the day as needed, and before I go to sleep at night.

A path to a remarkable you:

- Choose carefully what you say to yourself when things get tough.
- Choose to change your train of thought immediately if it's on the wrong track.
- Choose to have a growth mindset.
- Choose to operate with hopefulness.

Choose the courage you need to face the changes you will need to make. The daily things matter, including your actions, your thoughts, and even the words that are coming out of your mouth. It is in the courage to change the daily things the unmasking begins.

ABC

Call to Action

Continue using your journal.

Journal Prompt One

A

Action

1. What do you think is hindering you from becoming the best version of yourself?
2. What are your daily thoughts and actions? Which of those is keeping you attached to your wounds?
3. What do you hear yourself saying to yourself in times of frustration?

4. How do you see yourself when something goes wrong?

5. What do you allow others to say to you and over you?

Journal Prompt Two

B ___

Belief

1. Spend the next week keeping a word journal. Write out what you say and think to yourself.

2. When you review the list, what percentage are positive and what percentage of negative?

3. Are you being intentional or accidental with your words?

Journal Prompt Three

C ___

Choice

1. Create some turnaround statements with what you have discovered about your self-talk so far.

2. Rephrase and reframe those thoughts that come into your head or out of your mouth many times. I recite, "I know this could stop me, but it won't. I know that I can do this, simply one step at a time."

3. Create a "but" statement, one that you will use when you hear one of those accidental negative statements. It may be something like, "But I am more powerful than I know."

Growth does not happen all at once, nor does change. Over time you will see the number of negative statements declining and positive statements increasing. Lean in and make this a daily growth habit.

As you continue this journey and go through each chapter, you can start to reframe and re-mark different habits.

Sow a thought, reap an action.

Sow an action, reap a habit.

Sow a habit, reap a character.

Sow a character, reap a destiny!

Essential Item Two

Your Inner Circle Matters

A big part of success in this journey is the environment you create for yourself. More importantly, choose wisely those you travel with on this journey, those you spend time with, admire and emulate. These people play a big role in determining your environment and how you will keep going. Your inner circle is about who you allow close to you to speak into your life and influence you. A negative inner circle will bury you and a positive inner circle will empower you because they help you to see more than you can see yourself.

If you are spending time with people who are making wrong decisions and have bad attitudes, that will not empower you. I shared more about this in *Remarkable You* when I encouraged readers to look at their inner circle. Understanding who was in my inner circle and why they were there was a big lesson for me when I first started my journey. There is a great proverb that says,

Become wise by walking with the wise; hang out with fools and watch your life fall to pieces

(PROVERBS 31:20 MSG).

Simple advice but important truth. This advice caused me to pause and look deeply at my boundaries and the people I let into my circle of influence over my life and my journey.

Sometimes you admire someone for all the wrong reasons and allow them to speak over you and lead you in ways that you know deep in your heart are not okay. For example, I allowed my boundaries to be crossed when my family and I became close to another family with kids about the same age as ours. Soon after meeting them, I found myself doing things that later I would regret: drinking heavily, treating my children poorly, and neglecting my marriage. This boundary-less relationship had such a damaging impact on me and, by default, my family. I was so unaware of how this woman's influence was impacting everything and everyone around me.

When you allow your values to be set by someone else, dangerous habits can develop quickly. Allowing this friend and her family to cross over my boundaries certainly contributed to me acting in unhealthy ways.

Boundaries can best be described as how emotionally close you let people get to you and the level of influence you allow them to have over your thoughts and beliefs. Setting a boundary is like drawing a mark in the sand that defines a relationship. Boundaries allow others to know just how much you are willing to give or take before you step out of the relationship. I almost lost myself in that relationship.

In ancient times, walls were erected around cities as a source of protection. They were intentionally built to keep wild animals and enemies at bay. Cities were surrounded by unscalable walls. These walls stood as a warning to those on the outside, essentially saying, "You will not be allowed in until we know you are safe. And don't try to sneak in—we have guards up on the watch tower." The people in these cities learned to trust the walls, gatekeepers, and watchmen for their protection. It was also everyone's job in the city to maintain and rebuild the walls as needed.

You may not live in a house surrounded by walls and a moat. So how do you build walls to protect yourself? The walls you build will be designed to keep you on track with your thoughts and words.

The building of these boundary walls starts with understanding your values. Values are the principles that guide your decisions and behavior. They are like the four cornerstones of your walled city. When those values are clearly established and put in place daily, they bring great benefits to you and others. Letting your values determine your boundaries is called values-based self-leadership. Values aren't just meant to keep you on the safe side of the path of right versus wrong. They are also meant to keep you on the side of wisdom.

Values are guiding principles for your behavior, actions, and decisions. They help ensure you behave in a way that matches who you want to be at your core. When you know your values and use those values to filter who you allow into your inner circle, they take up a stone and help you build that wall.

I am not saying you need to change out everyone in your life, nor do you need to establish those boundaries all at once. What I am saying is that you need to be aware of whether the people in your life are adding to your values or trying to lead you away from them. When you are with them and leave feeling depleted or conflicted by their values, they are value destroyers. But when they make you feel empowered to keep going on your journey, they are value builders.

Call to Action

Continue using your journal.

Journal Prompt One

A
Action

We often choose our friends and build relationships with people based on proximity, which is not always the best decision. It's important to consider who you spend your time with based on more than proximity.

It can become so easy to choose the people who are right there to build our inner circle with, especially when they enjoy the same activities. At the end of the day, your friendships shape who you're becoming. Jim Rohn says,

> You're the average of the five people you spend most of your time with.

1. Make a list of your five closest friends. Are they value adders or value destroyers?
2. Do you follow people on social media and include them in your inner circle, allowing what they share to influence your life choices?
3. Take the time now to get clear on your values.

Write a response to, "Am I becoming who I want to be or am I becoming who I'm around and following on social media?"

Journal Prompt Two

B
Belief

It's good to remember that there is a difference between being friendly to someone and being friends with someone. You can be friendly to anyone if it's safe, but those you are in friendship with are those who you walk with, sit with, and share meals with during every season and should be value builders. Value builders are those you trust to call you out if you're doing something that they know is against your values. Everyone won't fit into this category, and that's okay.

It's also important to remember that you don't have to share your story with everyone. It's valuable to consider first who they are and what they will do with what you share.

As you start to look closer and deeper at your inner circle, take your time to journal honestly on the answers to these questions:

1. Do your friends encourage you and see the greatness in you even when you don't see it?

2. Do your friends just echo your aggravations and negativity?

3. Do your friends speak to the best in you and challenge you to keep going?

4. Who are you allowing to shape your life?

5. Are there some friends that you need to set strong boundaries with?

Journal Prompt Three

C
Choice

It takes courage to look closely at the people who influence you. I know personally there have been two significant times when I allowed a friend way too much power over my life and allowed them to cross boundaries. One of these I shared above, one in *Remarkable You*. The second friendship was quite damaging as well, but the second time I came out wiser. Now I take my time to look closer at who I will bring into my close, inner circle.

At the end of the day, you want to be surrounded by friends who believe in greater things within you. Is this the case in your inner circle?

Spend time journaling on the following questions:

1. Do your friends hold you steady and encourage you when you hit despair?
2. Do your friends give you energy and help propel you forward until you see victory?
3. Do you stay in friendships knowing they are bad for you out of fear of being lonely?
4. Are your daily choices empowering your journey or eroding your journey?

Remember it's always a choice...

As iron sharpens iron, so one person sharpens another,

PROVERBS 27:17 (NIV),

warns us to be careful to choose friends who sharpen us and help us grow rather than slow us down.

Essential Item Three

Self-Care

I love this quote from Paulo Coelho: "It's okay if your heart needs more time to accept what your head already knows." In those moments when you heart needs to catch up to your head, stop, pause to catch your breath, and remind yourself that even in a marathon race, the runner stops for a water break. The runner may lose time in the race, but without stopping they will become dehydrated and not finish the race. For all of us on this journey, stopping to catch our breath is fine. We must rehydrate to keep going.

Self-care is paramount to help you keep going as you learn to live life unmasked. When you do not protect your spirit, your heart is no longer a safe harbor, and it becomes a violated, looted city. You become vulnerable to the lies and negative words that pass through your ears. Weariness and despair become your daily food and cause your boundary walls to crumble.

Taking time out to care for yourself can remind you and others that you and your needs are important too. Establishing a self-care routine will strengthen you and set boundaries that you are of value and that you value yourself. Self-care can contribute to long-term feelings of well-being.

We can easily convince ourselves that we can't be released from the everyday matters that demand our attention. We think we are the only ones that can complete the tasks ahead. We think we can't afford the time to rest and enjoy some self-care. For a long time, self-care was at the bottom of my to-do list, and you and I both know the items at the bottom never seem to get done.

I have learned the hard way that when I am exhausted and don't eat well, I am irritable and can be irrational, and my emotions can spill out everywhere.

I end up making decisions that are not based on my values.

Call to Action

Your A, B, and C of self-care are significant on this journey—simple but significant.

Journal Prompt One

A

Action

Continue using your journal to document your answers and to maybe taking or creating intentional action.

1. How much self-care do you allocate time for?
2. Is there a regular time out for you, even a short ten, twenty, or thirty minutes?
3. Has self-care been on the bottom of your list, beyond your reach?

Journal Prompt Two

B

Belief

1. How would your journey be better if you took time out to care for yourself?
2. What would that self-care look like for you? Is it making time to exercise or eat healthily, is it time in the sun with a cup of tea? Is it a warm bath with quiet music? Is it reading a book? You will know what recharges you.

Journal Prompt Three

C
Choice

I know it may feel like it's impossible to create a space and a time to recharge. But I know you can do it, and it will give you the energy you need to keep going.

I often get up early so I can sit quietly with a cup of tea and journal. This routine allows me to start my day with a little self-care. If you are not a morning person, maybe your self-care happens just before bed, when you stay up and sit quietly and reflect on your day.

1. What action can you take to create this self-care space?
2. What changes do you need to make to your schedule to make sure this happens?
3. Be specific on this one: What timeframe will you allow yourself to set this in place?
4. Move your self-care to the top of your weekly to-do list.
5. Be consistent in setting up your self-care time—consistency is key.
6. Review weekly what self-care works well for you and what you need to do the next week differently until you set in place a rhythm of self-care.

Warning, dear ones: When we get busy, we can be fooled into thinking that self-care is something we can drop to make room for other tasks we believe are more important. You are of great value, and care for you must be at the top of your list.

Self-care isn't about self-indulgence. It's about refreshing, rehydrating, and renewing our minds, bodies, souls, and spirits for this journey.

Essential Item Four

Defiant Joy

This essential item empowered my journey to unmask my life so much that I don't want you to race through it.

This essential item is defiant joy! It sounds like a bold statement, I know. But let me tell you: When joy is set loose, it empowers your journey like jet fuel. Ask yourself this question: What if joy is meant to be ours? There is a joy that is defiant, bold, and (dare I say) rebellious. This is the type of joy you experience in the face of circumstances that have tried to take you out.

We often think of joy as something that happens to us, but the truth is that joy is something that happens in us. Joy is an inner feeling. Happiness is an outward expression. Joy endures hardship and trials and connects with meaning and purpose. A person pursues happiness but chooses joy.

Joy is a specific, defiant choice. We choose joy like we choose a positive attitude. We choose joy like we choose to see possibilities, answers, and options. It takes defiance to believe and know and live out that brave belief that circumstance, uncertainties, wounds of pain, and trauma do not have the final word.

Denying the truth of your current reality is not the answer to defiant joy. Being fully present in what is happening and still finding joy is defiant joy. Joy is about being present to whatever may be coming our way, whether it's good or causes grief. Believing that sorrow and loss do not have the final word takes defiance. It requires a strength of a spirit of joy that must be nurtured. It means engaging our lives fully.

Amid all the distress and suffering in the world, it can feel foolish or even be seen as frivolous to have joy. Certainly, there is a time to grieve. There is a time to mourn. There is a time to know our loss, but that doesn't mean we can't have joy even in that painful knowing. Joy is the heartbeat of the life. Joy is what sustains us, it is our strength, and it's a powerful weapon on your journey to unmask and re-mark your life.

My joy was stolen as I witnessed my father's suicide, and again just a few hours later when my uncle raped me. It took me a long time to learn and an even longer time to realize the truth that circumstances, trauma, trials, work, people, and worldly stress do not have the right to steal my joy. I had to fight hard, very hard, to get my joy back.

So often, we quit choosing joy because the wounds have been too deep, or we expect someone else to be responsible for our joy. We expect our spouse or children, friends or boss, or teammates to make us feel joy in our lives. We give away the one thing we can control, our choice, and instead accept whatever we get from the rest of the world as a measure of happiness. Sometimes being a person of joy amidst our circumstances may seem impossible. It was for me until I took a stand on my journey to say, "Let the impossible commence."

The secret to defiant joy is that it has absolutely nothing to do with the circumstances in your life or in the world. Defiant joy does not depend on whether you feel happy. Defiant joy comes from knowing who you are and whose you are. My defiant joy is a choice that I must make every day. For me joy is an action that begins with thanksgiving and gratitude. Knowing that joy is my choice became such a powerful tool on my journey.

> **Joy is a flame that glimmers only in the palm of an open hand. Let me encourage you to open your hand and heart to joy in the small things around you.**

We all have them—those small moments or things that often go unnoticed or unappreciated either because we think they're insignificant or we take them for granted because we live in a culture that celebrates big accomplishments. But what if we made it a habit to embrace and celebrate the small things?

I encourage you to make the courageous choice to begin your journey to defiant joy!

Call to Action

Continue to use your journal.

Journal Prompt One

A ____

Action

1. What circumstances, negative comments, or people have been robbing you of joy? Why is that?
2. What action do you need to take to push stop on the joy stealers in your life?

Journal Prompt Two

B ____

Belief

1. Do you believe that you deserve joy?
2. Have you been waiting for someone to bring you joy?

3. What dictates your joy—do your emotions play a role in this?

4. How can you discipline your mind to master your emotions around joy?

Journal Prompt Three

C
Choice

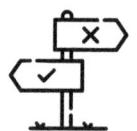

Take your time and be specific as you write out your responses to the following:

1. What would it look like, feel like, and/or be like if you looked for joy in your circumstances?

2. Let me add to that: What would it look like, feel like, and/or be like to walk in bold, defiant joy?

3. Write an action plan on how you will look for and walk in joy.

4. Use your journal to capture the plan and your daily joy moments. Remember, small steps over time lead to great change.

5. If the heights of our joy are measured by the depths of our gratitude, and gratitude is the way of seeing things, how often do you stop to think about what you are grateful for?

Real life is happening all around us. While we are waiting for the big things we hope will give us some sort of inner peace, contentment, or joy, the truth is that often the things that matter most are the small ones that are already present.

Let this hope burst forth within you, releasing a continual joy. Don't give up in a time of trouble, but commune with God at all times.

- ROMANS 12:1 TPT

Let me encourage you to choose joy, to fan the flame of joy, to look for it every day in the small things. You may just surprise yourself, as I did.

A joyful heart is good medicine, but a crushed spirit dries up the bones.

- PROVERBS 17:22 ESV

Brave and Courageous One ...

From my heart to your heart, dear one . . .

I know you feel broken beyond repair, that the wounds are way too deep to go on and the damage too great. Dear one, I truly feel your heart; I have sat in those feelings as well. I am telling you that as hard as it is to believe, you're not beyond repair, there is a way forward. Please don't give up. I know that within you is a brave, courageous heart that can take one more step. Just one more step. I know you can take that step and that with each step you take you will feel empowered to take more steps. I am praying for courageous strength for you for your journey as you step forward to re-mark your life. You are not alone.

I read a remarkable story of perseverance from the 2021 London Marathon. The *BBC News* article began, "Angie Hopson from Shropshire suffered what she thought was a muscle strain during training, but the pain became much worse during the race." Determined to raise money for Parkinson's research she battled on and finished the 26.2 mi (42 km) course. The following day she sat in urgent care explaining to the doctor that the pain began suddenly and sharply but was mild enough that she carried on, thinking it would work its way out. "By mile six," the story continued, "it was 'excruciating' and she had briefly stopped." Angie was determined to carry on and tried to power walk. At about mile nine a lady asked permission to walk with Angie, and stayed with her the remainder of race, offering encouragement and support along the way. "I think without her beside me it would have been very easy to stop," said Angie. The injured runner credited finishing the race to her fellow runner and to not knowing her leg was broken.

"Woman runs London Marathon with broken leg," BBC News, 21 October 2021, https://www.bbc.com/news/uk-england-shropshire-58840890.

We are each called to run our best race and to cross the finish line with the torch still burning bright in our hearts. Angie completed because she had a bigger purpose. Despite the pain she had to set her mind to take just one more step, then the next and to remain focused. She had to find enduring strength and discover staying power. Angie made a choice to hold onto hope, to walk past fear, and to keep going with bold purpose to cross that finish line.

> With each one of our steps we make a choice to turn our tears, our wounds, and our traumas into courage, to walk with hope, to walk into our healing victory.

The unmasking to re-mark race is a tough one, but it is the most worthwhile journey you will take. You will climb mountains and walk slowly through deep valleys. There will be times when you stumble, backslide, and have to retrace your steps to get back on track. Dear one, what counts in this race is not how fast you run, but that you tap into the courage that it takes for you to cross the finish line.

> **Courage is not the absence of fear; it's the will to persevere in the face of fear.**

This courage is there within you and will be essential on this journey.

At the end of each chapter, I have shared with you what steps I used to enable me to unmask on my journey and re-mark my life. These steps I shared can empower you to complete this journey if you take the actions. Hear my heart: Just as Angie had a cheerleader to help her finish her race, I am yours. I will be cheering you on, encouraging and coaching you to take the next step and keep going.

The power of choice is in your hands—the choice for the courage to walk fully into your destiny. Sometimes that courage may simply be getting out of bed and not giving up. Each time you look fear in the eye and say, "I see you" and step past it, that's another courageous step forward on your journey.

HG Wells asked, "What on earth would a man do with himself if something did not stand in his way?" He was saying that adversity is your friend, even when it feels like your enemy, and that life would be empty without some struggle. Every obstacle you face will reveal your strengths and weaknesses, shaping you and making you wiser and more confident.

The poet Ralph Waldo Emerson wrote:

> Whatever you do, you need courage. Whatever course you decide upon, there is always someone to tell you that you are wrong. There are always difficulties arising that tempt you to believe your critics are right. To map out a course of action and follow it to an end requires some of the same courage that a soldier needs. Peace has its victories, but it takes brave men and women to win them.

Now is the time for your victory—this is your time—this is your moment!

Knowing the battles that Joshua would have to fight to conquer the Promised Land, God told Joshua at three separate times, "Be strong and of good courage."

I encourage you to be strong and of good courage. Anytime you move forward, understand that obstacles will try to block your path, but like Joshua, you will prevail.

Please don't let anything or anyone stop you from living fully into your purpose, your destiny, or from creating the legacy that only you can create; this is in your hands. I believe in you. Use my belief in you until you can find your own if you need.

We have journeyed together through these pages where I have asked you to bravely make a choice to acknowledge your wounds, to grieve your grief, to believe you can courageously drop your masks to allow the healing process to begin. I have encouraged you to take the action that only you can take on your journey to healing.

Your strength comes in the power of your daily choices, your discipline, and your consistency. You have all the important tools you will need to succeed in your journey. Your actions will create ownership and momentum on this journey.

Words of wisdom for your daily choices to journey on:

- Change begins in you.
- Courage is within you.
- Courage's partner is action.
- Sometimes you can't change the circumstances you find yourself in, but you can change how you respond.
- Don't let what you can't do stop you from doing what you can.
- Your private decision will always have an effect beyond just you.
- As long as you make excuses, you won't be able to move forward.
- You can't remake your past, but you can make a new future.
- Focus on today. Today matters. Make today count.
- Know your values and use them as guardrails.
- It's never too late to be who you were called to be.
- Consistency is key.
- Forgiveness is essential.

I know that the only way to complete healing is to push through the pain. Don't allow the pain to be an anchor that weighs you down but use the pain as a tool to forge your path up the mountain and through the valleys. Healed wounds change our hearts, our life, our perspective, our confidence, and our future. Know that I am praying for each one of you that, as you turn the pages and work through the A, B, and C journal prompts, with each word you read and each action step you take, you will feel strengthened and empowered. Every step is taking you forward into a life that is healed and where you are living freely in who you are called to be.

Well done, dear one. You are truly brave and courageous. I am so very proud of you.

Epilogue: The X Factor

On November 6, 2011, two days after leaving my senior government position to start my own business, I sat in church listening to a guest preacher talking about the X factor. *Merriam-Webster's* Dictionary defines X factor as "a circumstance, quality, or person that has a strong but unpredictable influence." He spoke about his daughter Mikala. He said that, looking at her, she appeared small and insignificant according to world's standards. And, sadly, that's how her school friends treated her. Mikala had a great relationship with her dad and placed her trust in his guidance. He encouraged her to join a basketball team because he saw that she had a call on her life, a God-given purpose. He saw something in her that was special.

When she joined the basketball team, she was treated like she didn't belong by the coach and other team members. She sat on the bench for many games until the time they needed her to sub in. When she stepped onto the court, she excelled. Everything changed because of the X factor within her. She stepped out in faith and what was in her was activated.

He was talking about the X factor of God, the light within that causes transformation to occur. This X factor is activated by stepping out in faith, moving forward, and taking action. It is to walk in the persona God has created within each one of us.

Mikala became the most valuable player and took a losing team to a champion team. What was in Mikala was a God-given purpose, but it required courage to step into and trust in God's purpose for her life.

While I sat listening to his words, playing over in my mind on a loop was, "I don't believe that I have any value in any way. There is nothing of value, no X factor within me." I believed these lies. I was a member of a church where I was encouraged to see more within myself, to seek God and to trust Him. I was told by some members of the congregation that there was a call on my life to be a woman of influence. But honestly, I could not believe this was possible. I found it easier to pretend to have faith than to unmask and share the truth of who I really was inside. Wounds, trauma, and a life filled with grief and pain caused me to doubt God's goodness and especially His goodness to me. I liked the community of the church, but I didn't have a relationship with Jesus. Everything changed for me that day on my floor when I reached out in final desperation to God. He rescued me from my suicidal plan. If this God cared enough to show me that my life mattered, I wanted to find out more.

Trusting God was a difficult journey for me, requiring me to let go of my past, learn to forgive those that wounded me so deeply, and forgive myself. After my trust and my innocence were ripped away by those that were meant to love me, I lost all ability to trust. My father took me to the darkest places in my life. The wounds he placed in me almost cost me my life. My uncle's love was rape, and my mother's love was neglect and aunt's comfort was shame. Nothing inside of me could make sense of trust, and the idea of trusting this unknown God that people told me about seemed impossible. Yet He loved me enough to step in and rescue me when I cried out in desperation to Him. I needed to dig deep for courage to make this choice of trust.

I started sitting with my journal and my Bible, going through the Psalms and the chapters that revealed to me who I am to God and who He is for me. I learned that He loves me unconditionally, that there is nothing I can do to stop Him from loving me. But it was a choice on my part to reach out to Him as I did on my floor that day. I spent many, many hours journaling on the character of God, His faithfulness, His grace, and His love for me.

As I read the words in the Bible, they revealed to me that God is able to do immensely more than I could ever ask or imagine (Ephesians 3:20) and that I am part of His plan, a plan with hope and a future for my life (Jeremiah 29:11). I saw that there is an X factor, a God-given purpose within me that was activated when I simply invited Jesus into my heart. I prayed simple prayers and asked for understanding, strength, and wisdom. God enabled me to recognize His truth as I committed my life to Jesus.

This journey that I continue today has settled in my heart without a doubt that I can trust the promises, the grace, and the love of my Heavenly Father. I discovered that He loved me so much that He sent His son Jesus as a sacrifice on the cross for me so I could have life (John 3:16).

The world around us is a crazy place, replete with pandemics, wars, death, pain, and heartache. It may be hard to fathom a God that is love, and it certainly was for me. Dear one, His heart is for us. He wants to impart to us His resilience, which is what we need to take this journey to complete healing.

As I open my heart to invite Jesus in, it has opened me up to be led and guided by Him each and every step forward, growing me stronger on this journey. I still needed to take my action steps, my A, B and C's, as I walked into freedom, but in taking those steps forward, I knew Jesus was with me all the way.

Whenever I found myself struggling to forgive those who had been responsible for those bitterly painful, damaging experiences, I was able to ask God to help me forgive. When I struggled to take the next step, I asked Him for the strength to prevail. The God I know now is a God of restoration. A God that redeems our past and our regrets, He has shown me that He is the God of impossibilities. He has shown me the X factor that is within me.

There is a God-given purpose within you, an X factor that is just waiting to be let loose in your life. It's a choice you can make to ask Jesus into your heart. It's a simple prayer, turning your heart to God, asking Jesus to come into your heart and be the Lord of your life. He knows you, loves you, and values you. Your past no longer defines your future.

The world bombards us every day, dear one, telling us that we are not enough, telling us that our wounds, our trauma, our griefs will keep us trapped. That we won't measure up. Beneath this bombardment of our busy and besieged lives, our hurting hearts are searching for hope, the hope that comes from God.

When our hearts are hurting, our hope is not shaken. When our hearts ache from what we see, we can still trust in God. He is the hope that holds us and gives us the strength to prevail.

My gracious God took my heart, which was broken, and filled with excruciating pain, and led me on a journey of healing. Because I was willing to take one step and then the next, God has used my life to walk alongside those that are wounded and damaged by life. Do you see the incredible beauty of this? The very things the enemy used to try to take me out, to destroy my life, are the very things that God has used from my life to empower others to victory. The X factor!

I know God the Father is just waiting for you to ask His Son, Jesus, to come into your life and journey with you. It's a choice that only you can make, dear one.

Following is a paraphrase by Christine Caine of verses from Luke 15 that reflect God's infinite grace, paraphrased:

No matter how deep the pit, I will always seek you and rescue you because I love you with everlasting love.

Even when you mess up, even when you're careless or mistaken or afraid or broken or weak, even when you deliberately sin, I still love you.

Even when you're incapable of doing anything for anyone or even helping yourself, I still love you.

I come for all those that make mistakes, those that are overlooked, devalued and despised. I come for the lost, whether the lost is a silly sheep, a silver coin, a squandering son ... or you.

He always searches for the one that is lost!

In closing, I want to share my favorite Psalm, 139:1–6 from The Passion Translation, that guides me back to His strength. May it do the same for you.

Lord, you know everything there is to know about me.

You perceive every movement of my heart and soul,

and you understand my every thought before it even enters my mind.

You are so intimately aware of me, Lord.

You read my heart like an open book and you know all the words I'm about to speak before I even start a sentence!

You know every step I will take before my journey even begins.

You've gone into my future to prepare the way, and in kindness you follow behind me to spare me from the harm of my past.

With your hand of love upon my life, you impart a blessing to me.

This is just too wonderful, deep, and incomprehensible!

Your understanding of me brings me wonder and strength.

Journey well, my precious one... ♡
I am praying for you.
Love, Wendy

I would love to hear from you and how you are going on your journey.

Please don't hesitate to reach out to me to let me know.

About the Author

Hi, I am Wendy Burns, wife to Bill and mother and grandmother of amazing children and grandchildren that all bring such joy to my life.

I am a fervent believer in the power of choice in a person's life. It such a powerful tool in the process of breaking free from old patterns of thinking and behaviors that hold them back from living in their true purpose.

As a transformational coach, I work with executives, leaders, individual women, and women's groups to enable them to understand the importance of self-leadership. As part of the journey of self-leadership I work closely with women to help them find their voice and empower their lives.

I am the author of *Remarkable You*, my first book, also I speak on professional topics such as leadership and empowering women as well as an inspirational speaker on the topics of suicide, domestic violence, alcoholism, and sexual assault from the point of a survivor having intimate, first-hand experience in these areas. My life exemplifies resilience and the ability to reshape and reclaim brokenness into a life brimming with purpose and love.

One More Thing

Before you close this book and put it on the shelf, may I ask you a favor?

If you found any part of this book helpful or inspirational, please consider leaving a review on Amazon.

Your review is not so much for me, although I have to say it is a blessing to receive; rather, it serves as a guide to someone just like you—someone who is searching for the key to unmask and step into their remarkable journey.

Thank you

Let's Stay Connected

To take a deeper dive into *Unmask: Stop Hiding, Start Living*, visit:

www.wendyburnsconsulting.com.au

To hire Wendy Burns as a coach, workshop leader, or speaker contact Wendy at

wendy@wendyburnsconsulting.com.au

For discount bulk purchases of this book for your organization or conferences please email the publisher at

info@SkinnyBrownDogMedia.com

Unmask: Stop Hiding, Start Living has an accompanying journal available with online book retailers.

www.ingramcontent.com/pod-product-compliance
Lightning Source LLC
Chambersburg PA
CBHW051615010526
44107CB00037B/1437/J